LOVE YOURSELF

HOW TO END THE HURTING AND START BUILDING SELF ESTEEM, CHARISMA AND CONFIDENCE

JONATHAN GREEN

Paperback ISBN-13: 978-1718792197

Paperback ISBN-10: 1718792190

Before you can love me, you must first love yourself.

DON'T GO IT ALONE

The hardest part of dealing with depression is going it alone. When you are in isolation, the night can seem so dark. Please join my FREE, private Facebook group filled with supportive people on the same path.

https://servenomaster.com/lovely

INTRODUCTION

I was six years old the first time I thought about committing suicide. I felt that my parents didn't give me enough attention and took me for granted; I didn't feel like I fit in my family the way that children on TV and the kids from school did. I felt distant from everyone, and I had a perfect plan. I would climb onto the roof of the house on Christmas morning before my parents woke up, and I would jump off. That would show them. I had this dream of getting revenge on my parents, and I imagined the look on their faces when they realized they didn't appreciate me enough, as they carted me off to my funeral. In my vision and in my imagination, of course, I was always there to watch everything, like an invisible ghost. Otherwise, what's the point?

As I grew older, I began to realize that I wouldn't actually be there – I wouldn't get to watch it, and smashing into the ground would probably really, really hurt. It took me a long time to discover that the force affecting me, this curse on my life had a name. Depression. It's an overwhelming force, and people who have never had it have no understanding of it. They think it's just sadness or perhaps just big sadness. If you are like me and you have dealt with this problem, you know it's much more, and it can become this monster of a problem you don't know how to deal with.

I never thought I would write a book about depression. I have recorded a few podcast episodes on the topic, and I have blogged about it, but it's not my main area. My followers are mostly entrepreneurs or people who want to succeed in building their businesses, but when you work alone, depression is more of a dangerous force because there is no one around. There is no one to check your depression or notice from the outside that something is going wrong. When you are alone, depression is a lot more sinister, and it can accomplish a lot more. You are already in isolation, which is depression's favorite way to start taking control.

I have decided to put together this book for these reasons. Whether you are working for yourself or not, you can join me on the journey of how I overcame depression and how you can accomplish the same thing.

A NOTE ABOUT LINKS

Throughout this book I mention other books, images, links, and additional content. All of that can be found at:

https://servenomaster.com/loveyourself

You don't have to worry about trying to remember any other links or the names of anything mentioned in this book. Just enjoy the journey and focus on taking control of your destiny.

1

EVERYBODY HURTS

There have been so many moments in my life where I felt like I wasn't good enough – I felt like I had nothing to offer the world and I would never fit in. As a child, I struggled greatly to learn how to socialize, and I didn't make any friends until I was seventeen. At best, I had a few "frenemies" when I was younger, but there were always frictions and complications. If you have read my book about depression, you know that I faced a lot of emotional challenges when I was younger. But in this book, we are going to go beyond that.

We are going to talk about what happens when we interact with other people. If you are anything like me, you have been hurt a lot in your life; you've had people say words that hurt. As a child, everybody's heard over and over again, "Sticks and stones may break my bones, but words will never hurt me," or, "I'm rubber, you're glue, whatever you say bounces off me and sticks to you." We use these little magical phrases to mask how much people's words can hurt. But it's not just other people's words; sometimes, I'm my own harshest critic. I look in the mirror, and I don't like what I see. I question my skills as an author, as a teacher, as a businessman, and as an entrepreneur all the time. Sometimes, I wonder if I'm a good enough father.

These thoughts flicker through my head. I want to be totally honest with you in this book. I believe in leading from the front, so I will share some very personal things about myself first to make you feel more comfortable facing your inner disappointments. Sometimes I look at my kids and think, "Am I already behind?" My daughter is four years old; she only speaks three languages. Could I have done better? What else could I have done? My son is fifteen months old, and he can only swim with floaties. Why can't he swim without floaties yet?

If you know a bit about languages and swimming, you know that both of my children are very advanced; yet these kinds of thoughts worm their way into my head at times. That is because most of our judgments concerning ourselves are not based on rationality or reality; they are just poisonous thoughts floating in our head. They are little whispers. They are designed to hurt you, not to educate you. Those little babbling thoughts are not going to help me as a father. They limit me.

In this book, we are going to fix this issue together. In fact, we are going to go beyond that, and I am very excited. This book is about more than just learning to fall in love with yourself; it's about learning to teach the rest of the world to fall in love with you too. And we are going to help you build some powerful skills and assets. We are going to build your confidence, self-esteem, and charisma. These are some ambitious goals, but I like to shoot big.

Shoot for the stars and, if you fail, you will hit the moon. Guess what? No one has been to the moon since the 70s. It's ripe for the taking. We've stopped shooting for the stars. Despite all the talk about colonizing Mars, I'd settle for a trip to the moon. I'd love to see what the moon looks like in HD, and I'd love to see some iPhone shots of the moon. Will the iPhone work in a vacuum? I'd love to find out. I don't think it needs air, but maybe all Apple products need oxygen to breathe.

I want you to think the same way about yourself.

Let's shoot for some crazy goals. Let's make things happen – let's make you a super confident superstar who believes in themselves. Let's go beyond that, and let's make you charismatic. Charisma is where you say things and other people get excited; they are drawn to you magnetically because your personality has the force of gravity.

Intrapersonal Skills: What Are They, and Why Are They Important?

As we dig into this book, we are going to do a lot of cool things together, and we are going to start by assessing where you are right now. We need to understand who you are and dig into your emotions and motivations. What we are going to look at is your intrapersonal skills.

Intrapersonal skills are your ability to measure and assess yourself, to look at your feelings, your motivation, your way of thinking, and your life. This is the ability to look at yourself and go, "I'm depressed," "I'm not depressed," "I'm happy," "I'm not happy." There is no tool that a doctor can use to measure your level of happiness if you don't talk. This is why the psychiatrist's worst nightmare is someone who doesn't speak; they have no idea what's going on, and there is nothing they can do to help. Just as with gravity, psychologists can only study the effect of your emotions, but they cannot look at them directly. They can only see how your emotions affect your words, and your words tell them what's happening.

This book is about self-awareness and self-management; self-awareness is understanding, and self-management is taking control of the operation. By the end of this book, you are going to have complete control of the operation. We are going to fire all those crappy middle managers that have been messing up your emotional business for too long.

Let's look at some examples of intrapersonal skills, and as you assess yourself, I want you to look at where you are along this spectrum. It is worth writing your answers down in your Love Yourself Journal.

1. Do you have a deep understanding of your own thought processes and motivations? Do you know why you do things? If you have a day you feel sad, do you know why you feel sad? If the sadness ends, can you understand why it ended and what caused it to end? Do you feel like a ship at sea being tossed by the storm of emotions and winds of nature? Or do you understand where those winds are coming from?

2. Do you monitor your thinking and motivations, and do you actively reject negativity? This is the key step. This is a bit of self-management. When you notice yourself getting depressed, angry or confused, do you take action? Or are you like me and my dad when we get lost, we will do anything other than ask for directions? Do you simply accept the negative that is happening and wait for the storm to end?

3. Do you avoid negative and destructive thought processes? Sometimes we have physical triggers. For instance, one of my negative thought processes is that I love to snack; I cannot control some of my eating behaviors. If you've seen pictures of me or the negative fan mail I occasionally get, my weight is often a centerpiece of those discussions. If there is a snack in my house, I do not have the ability to resist it. I am aware of this. This is why there are no snacks in my house. There is not a single bag of chips, and there are no tins of cookies. None of the things that I cannot resist are there. Everyone else in my family is skinny; my wife and my children are in great health. Part of that is because the kids have her genes, and part of it is because they have my fear of them suffering the same weight problems I have.

Whenever I notice a negative thought trying to creep into my brain, I take action to resist. Do you do the same kinds of things? If you notice yourself getting fat and depressed, do you take action? If you read my book about depression, you know that when depression attacks, I immediately tell someone and do something fun to fight against it. If you have read *Overcoming Depression* and are taking action, then you can say "yes" here. But if you are someone who lets the negativity wash over you and take control, then you are currently stuck at "no."

4. Do you have the ability to visualize effectively? Do you have the ability to imagine a goal, a desire, or something you want in front of you and hold it there long enough for it to affect you? Or do those visualizations seem ephemeral? Do they seem like a memory of a ghost?

5. Are you good at internal decision-making and problem-solving? Can you look at a problem within yourself and take action to improve it? Can you see that you have a negative pattern, behavior, or thought cycle and find a solution?

6. How would you rate yourself on a scale of 1 to 10 for mindfulness? Mindfulness is the ability to live in the moment and only think about the "right now." This is where you don't think about yesterday, and you don't think about tomorrow; you don't regret past decisions, and you don't worry about what will come next. You are too busy living.

Another element of mindfulness is looking at how people use technology. I don't take a lot of pictures anymore; in fact, I have to make an active decision to bring my camera. We have so many cameras in my house, and every phone in the house has cameras. We are such a camera-happy family, and yet it's not how I like to live; I don't want to live my life through a lens. I want to be right there in the moment. I'd rather see my child swim and hold him in my arms than take a thousand pictures of him swimming. Are you living in the moment? Or are you trapped in the past? Do you experience life through technology?

7. Do you avoid counterproductive thinking and behavior? A counterproductive behavior would be to buy snacks and put them in the house; I'd be fighting against myself. It's like putting landmines inside your house; don't do that. But maybe you do things that tempt yourself. If you are a person who struggles with alcohol, a counterproductive behavior would be saying, "I could just have one." It is the most common refrain of the relapser. One will be fine; it won't be a big deal. And this is a disease I have dealt with in my family; I am aware of the experience because I have been around it a lot. Do you find yourself dreaming about things you know are bad for you?

8. Do you have the ability to think deeply? Are you someone who is stuck on the surface? A way to see how deeply you think is to look at what someone says when you are talking to someone. Does it ever cross your mind to wonder why they said it?

There is a classic scene from an old movie that gets repeated a lot because it is funny; someone has to get rid of their dog, and so they pretend to hate the dog to make it leave. The dog is sad, and the kid keeps yelling and has to throw a rock, and the dog finally leaves. If you look at the surface of this moment, you think, "Wow, that kid hates this dog." But if you knew the context and looked a little deeper, you would see the thought behind the action. You would see that maybe his neighbor was going to kill his dog, so the kid had to hide the dog to save its life or something similar.

Do you ever look at the "why" behind the things people say to you?

THINK about these questions and let's take an action step here. Grab a notebook. I want you to call this the Love Yourself Journal. If you are super techy, you might want to do this on your tablet, or some other device on your phone. But I like to do this by hand. What we are dealing with here is a mental problem. All of these fears, anxieties, and stresses are in the mind. Lack of confidence and charisma all happen within your head. We need to fight these issues where they are weakest: outside your body.

Doing that through physical action is more empowering. The more "in the real world" your solution, the easier this process will be. Write down your answers to these different questions. Assessing your personal skills will help you with where you are right now. You can work your way through the activities in your Love Yourself Journal, and at the end, you will have a written text of where you started your journey and where you ended up.

Intrapersonal Intelligence Test

We have looked at some big picture questions, and now we are going to zoom in. We started with the forest; now let's look at the trees. I have put together some very specific questions for you to answer. Let's measure your current intrapersonal intelligence level.

1. How good are you at being alone? Do you enjoy your own company?

a) I do enjoy my own company, and I enjoy being alone sometimes.

b) I almost always find it difficult to be alone.

2. Are you good at keeping track of your thinking and derailing nega-tive thinking?

a) I'm quite good at this.

b) Not usually.

3. Generally, how strong is your ability to control your thinking processes?
    a) Strong or very strong.
    b) Not very strong or weak.

4. When you have negative feelings about yourself, how good are you at dismissing them and choosing a positive route, instead? In other words, how good are you at being kind to yourself?
    a) Good or very good.
    b) Not very good.

SCORING: THE MORE "A" answers you chose, the better developed your intrapersonal skills are. If you chose lots of "b" answers, don't worry! We are all fully capable of improving our intrapersonal abilities.

WRITE down your score in your Love Yourself Journal. I want you to remember that score because as we move forward, we will improve it. No matter where you are at, we are going to help you get better. And by the end of this book, we are going to help you get a lot better.

Reflection Questions

What I'd like you to do now is reflect on the following five questions and add your answers to your Love Yourself Journal. With these reflection questions, try to connect with your deepest thoughts.

1. How well do you know yourself right now? What steps do you plan on taking to get to know yourself a little bit better?

2. What are your three best qualities?

3. Right now, do you love yourself? Be honest with me, you can write yes or no, or maybe you need to give yourself a spectrum, like you love yourself eighty-seven percent. But here is another question, how well do you think it would go down if I told my wife I love her eighty-seven percent?

If your answer right now is "no," look in a mirror or look into your soul and ask yourself, "Why not?" What is holding you back? Maybe there are things you have done in the past or decisions you regret, and the past has a hold on you. Or maybe you are not where you want to be in your life yet, so you look at the future, and it's not quite where you want it to be. Dig into it, and ask yourself what's wrong. Is it your personality? Is it the people around you? What's missing?

4. On a scale of 1 to 10, how do you rate your confidence and self-esteem? How much do you believe in yourself and how much do you believe in your ability to take action? Do you believe you can effectively deal with the challenges and problems that life throws your way?

5. Do you consider yourself to be charismatic? Why or why not? On a scale of 1-10, rate your charisma.

6. As a final thought, do you think that improving your self-confidence and self-esteem will lead to an increase in your charisma?

ANSWER THESE REFLECTION QUESTIONS; be proactive. This is an active book, and this is the future. Fill in your sections and when you finish writing your answers in your Love Yourself Journal, and only then, join me in the next chapter.

2

TALKING TO YOURSELF

Now you have a better idea of what we are going to work on in this book and the power of intrapersonal skills. You may be wondering how you can develop these skills; how can anyone improve their personality? These are critical questions because they are the centerpiece of this journey we are taking together.

In order to have a truly satisfying and fulfilling life, strong intrapersonal skills are critical. Many people think that intrapersonal skills are a talent – something you are born with; either you have it, or you don't. But a skill is actually a learned and strengthened ability; it is something that we can improve. That difference is incredibly important.

When I was younger, many areas of my life where I was weak, I assumed were talents. I assumed that you were born with a good or a bad personality, popular or unpopular, happy or sad. I thought there was nothing I could do about it, and that was dead wrong; anyone can make the decision to improve their thought life – their intrapersonal skills. It simply requires a bit of dedication and reflection, but the efforts will be worth it.

When you strengthen you thought life – when you become your

own biggest fan and finally *fall in love with yourself again* – you gain some amazing results, including greater self-awareness, a better sense of control over your own mental well-being, a better sense of control of your own life, greater confidence, a greater level of kindness towards yourself, a true sense of wisdom and deeper insights, a better sense of your own intelligence, and a greater ability interact with other people.

Before we can have great communication and great connections with other people, before we can form emotional bonds and meet other people, we have to truly understand and fall in love with ourselves. That is the first step on the path to greatness.

Methods for Improving Your Intrapersonal Awareness

As with any area we want to develop, I want to give you multiple tools and techniques that you can use. I have an extensive list of methods that you can use to improve your intrapersonal skills, and you're going find some of them easy and others challenging. You have to go outside your comfort zone. I don't expect you to implement every single one of these methods every day for the rest of your life; this isn't how we find success. What we want to find are the techniques that work for you – the techniques that you enjoy using, that you find success with, and that you can see yourself implementing in the long run.

What I do ask is that you try each of these techniques at least twice. Sometimes you have a bad experience the first time you try something, so I ask you to try everything twice to be sure we find the absolute best techniques for you. As we work our way through these methods, you're going to find the perfect personal mix of techniques to give yourself the insights you have always looked for.

1. Regular meditation

Self-awareness is one of the critical steps along this path. The way to become more self-aware is to silence our surface level thoughts for a moment and give the rest of our brains a chance to dig deep and see what's going on. You might have some preconceptions about meditation, but I ask you to put them aside; just give it a shot. Meditation isn't about emptying up your mind and leaving yourself vulnerable to random thoughts; it is the exact opposite. True meditation is about blocking negative thoughts about the past and the future.

We spend most of our time thinking about things we can no longer change or things that will never happen. When you enter a state of meditation, you remove those extraneous parts and focus on things that actually matter. You become more in touch with how you're truly feeling and what's happening in the moment. You don't have to practice any particular form of meditation or repeat a special phrase; it can be as simple as sitting down, turning off all distractions, and focusing on your body.

Begin by sitting still and noticing your breathing. Pay attention to how the breath enters and leaves your lungs. Slow down and take control of your breathing. This is a process that we are so used to, we treat it as something automatic like a heartbeat, but in fact, you have control over your breath. Take a moment to just be in control of your body and pay attention to how that feels. Stop thinking about the past, don't think about the future; just think about doing this process correctly. Give all of your attention to doing something right. In that moment, you will know everything is right; you will experience the first glimmers of mindfulness. In this state, you will notice that your mental clutter begins to disappear; you can more accurately gauge your inner thought life and how you truly feel about things.

Meditation ignites the process of taking dominion over your mind. In the West, many of us give special powers to emotions. Our culture, some medical professions, and most media treat emotions like magical powers that can completely control us, as though the emotion can make you do things like a puppet on a string. These are impressive legal defenses, but it's all just smoke and mirrors. You are in control of your emotions. Emotions are simply thoughts. Taking back control of your mind and reasserting your dominance begins with mindfulness.

2. Keep a Personal Reflective Journal

Hopefully, you have already started a Love Yourself Journal, where you're going to write down the answers to the quiz questions, your reflective thoughts, and your experiences throughout this journey. But even after you finish this book, you should continue to write down how things make you feel. We are notoriously terrible at remembering our experiences. If I ask you a month from now how you were feeling today, there's a ninety-nine percent chance you will not remember, unless you write it down.

We all have revisionist memories that change how we perceive things over time, and our memories adjust. The only way to have an accurate record of your journey is to write it down. We want to control how you remember the past, so you can track yourself as you improve. Journaling has helped me through many processes. I have been through points where six months into a transformation, I feel like a total failure, but I look at myself at the beginning of the journey, and I realize I'm already at a point I never thought I would achieve.

Things I had never dreamed of achieving have become my bad days, and when I look at my past, I can only see my trajectory because I wrote it down. Instead of assuming, you have proof that you've climbed a mountain and you're doing some amazing things.

Oftentimes we feel impotent in our culture; we feel like our actions don't lead to anything, and we don't have the ability to affect the outcome of our lives. Writing down your experiences, how you feel, and the things you accomplish will remind you that you are in the driver's seat. You'll begin to feel a greater sense of control, and your reality will come into sync with your thought life. Right now, if you feel like you're not very effective, your confidence is not very high, and you are not sure how to truly love yourself, you are most likely lacking congruency. Congruency is where your inside life and your outside life, your mind and your body, are matched up. The greater your congruency, the stronger your mental barriers become.

We can only develop this skill when we truly understand what's happening and we have a good record.

The purpose of a journal is not for it to become homework or an added stress in your life. Most people hate the first week of journaling, and a month later, it becomes a critical part of life that you could never imagine not doing. Journaling will become a part of your life you are excited about. You have to put in a little effort at first, but then it develops its own sense of motion, and it becomes something to look forward to, to see how well you've done. You begin to look at your life as a score board; you are excited to see all the things you've accomplished every day.

3. Actively Boost Your Self-Esteem

We do so many things throughout the day that don't feel good. There are people who see the glass half-full, people see the glass half-empty, and then there are witty people that joke about it and try to create a third answer. The idea is to measure your self-talk where you range on the scale from pessimism to optimism. Most people justify their pessimism and negative thought patterns by calling it realism, but it's not.

If you struggle with this, we can use the Love Yourself Journal to be effective: every time you have a negative thought about something that might happen, write it down. After a week, look at the predictions your brain has made, and circle all the ones that came true. You will discover that your brain is horribly ineffective at predicting the future; ninety-nine percent of the time you will be dead wrong, and you will realize that pessimism is not realism at all. Give yourself credit and permission to feel good about things. When you accomplish something, celebrate it, no matter how small it is.

When you celebrate small processes, then you enjoy the journey. If you are only allowed to celebrate when you complete something, if you decide then you can only be satisfied when you finish reading this whole book, then you will probably fail, or at least you will certainly not enjoy the process. If you create artificial standards, you won't succeed. Reward yourself for the small steps, and you'll be training your brain to enjoy the process. If every time you slip up your focus on the failure rather than the success, then you attach a negative emotion to the act of trying. You train yourself to not try, but if you say you have tried your best instead, you're going to do better next time.

If you act for yourself like that great buddy in the weight room who helps you lift the weights, or the boxer's friend in the corner who shouts, "You can do it champ, one more round and you've got him!" then you can become your own biggest fan, your own biggest supporter. Begin to eliminate negative self-talk, stop saying things like, "I'm worthless," "I'm a loser," "I'm useless," "I give up forever." These negative thoughts don't lead anywhere; it's empty statements. Every time you notice yourself saying one of these things, say "Stop! I'm not doing that anymore. I'm not useless."

4. Spend More Time with People Who Make You Feel Good About Yourself

I've had a few people in my life who made me feel bad about myself. Sometimes it's because these people are bullies, and when we are younger, we face that a lot. There are people who push us down to make themselves feel good, but sometimes we are around people who make us feel bad simply because they have low self-esteem.

Misery loves company, and they love bringing you down. If you have people in your life that want to compete with you and feel the need to keep you from flying too close to the sun, spend some time away from them. When you spend too much time with someone like that, you lose your sense of self-esteem and your sense of reality. That person can take control of you, and we don't want any of that to happen.

Change the people you spend time with, and you can change your experience of life. If you spend your time with people that are always happy, you become happy all the time. They will pull you up to their emotional level. We become similar to the people we spend the most time with, so why not spend time with people that you actually want to be like?

5. Treat Yourself

You need to be on your own side, and you should reward yourself when you do good. That does not mean eating a pie, ice cream or cake every time you accomplish something, but it does mean giving yourself a pat on the back, a sticker, or permission to feel good – whatever rewards work for you based on your situation. Put some healthy rewards in place that encourage you to do well. In your Love Yourself Journal, if you have the version that I prepared for you, you'll notice that there are spots on every page where you can add stickers to give yourself a little bit of encouragement. Nothing makes a journal more fun than a few stickers.

6. Write a Plan for Your Personal Development

As you go through this book, I am going to give you tools, techniques, and a strategy for the future, but you have to start acting now. Begin thinking of what you would like to accomplish and where you would like to be in six months, three months, or even three weeks. Set specific, measurable and manageable goals, develop a plan and say, "This is what I want to be like in six months. I will have no more negative thoughts. I want to be charismatic, and I will have three new friends to believe in me."

Be specific and be bold; wish for big things, and they will come true. When you implement that plan and get the results you desired, your sense of self-control will go through the roof because you accomplished a goal. It turns out you can plan and accomplish great things.

8. Build Some Quiet Time in Your Life

This can be something more than meditation. Sometimes, especially when we are low on the self-confidence tree, we do everything we can to fill our life with noise because we are afraid of the thoughts in the back of our head. I used to live a very loud life. I would sleep with music blasting, I would watch TV all the time, and I would always be around people because I was afraid to be alone with myself. I was afraid of the voices in the back of my head and the bad things they were saying about myself.

We are moving beyond that now, and we are beginning to take dominion over our thought life, so that every day you can have a quiet time. You just look at your day and take a moment to breathe. We spend all day experiencing; take a moment to assess your experiences. Reconnect with yourself; listen to what your body and your mind are telling you.

9. Create a Reward Ritual

Rituals can be very powerful, and they can help us to get into different emotional states. I use rituals in many areas of my life. I start my day with a ritual to get myself in the right mood for work, and when I'm about to sit down and write I have a preparation ritual to empty my mind of distracting thoughts and just focus on my writing; it helps me to be very fast and skillful with my words. Getting into the perfect emotional states with rituals helps me to be a better writer, and it can also help you to get into a positive, high-self-confidence emotional state.

Your ritual can be getting massage or putting together a process where you watch your favorite show. Many people, especially groups of people who love a particular show, have an entire ritual for how they watch it. They get together with their friends on a Saturday night, and everyone brings their own food. The host makes sure drinks are provided, and everyone sits down to watch the show together and then discuss it afterward. This is a ritual around a television show, which maybe you've done or haven't done, but at least you are familiar with this idea.

Build the same thing in your life. Build rituals that are just about you spending time with you and feeling good. It can be just you doing an activity that you enjoy on your own, and it can be a physical activity or a mental activity.

There are certain activities that I find very cathartic because they induce a sense of peace with myself. I've always struggled with exercise, and yet I love surfing, stand-up paddling, and kayaking. Sometimes, when I feel the stress of the day, I take my kids to swim in the pool, and I'm so busy with them requiring one hundred percent of my attention that I cannot think about anything else; their safety is on the line, so they get all of my focus. It clears my mind, and I find it very relaxing. I swim with my children every day, and it keeps me in a perpetual state of calm and relaxation. It feels good.

10. Set Goals and Follow Through on Them

You need to experience accomplishing things. As much as we are talking about mental processes, we don't want to fight our mental problems where they are strong; we want to fight them where they are weak. We want to fight them in the real world, and in the world outside your body, it's very easy to feel fulfilled when you accomplish things.

Rather than take you through a bunch of mental exercises that make you feel really good, let's do things and feel good because you've done them; then the proof is absolute, there's no possibility for doubt to enter your mind because with a real goal, it's a "yes or no" at the end. Either you didn't do it, or you did.

Set both short-term and long-term goals. Oftentimes, we set these big overarching New Year's resolutions that we will never achieve because they are so far away. "I want to lose 174 pounds." That takes two or three years; it's too hard. Most people fail because they aim so far away it's beyond the horizon; you cannot see it anymore.

If you set ten small goals for tomorrow, you will probably complete all ten. Start by breaking your goals into small pieces that you can achieve. I have small goals that I try to achieve every day; I try to exercise for an hour every day, swim with my children least once every day, put out a podcast episode every weekday, and so on. I have a mix of health, work, and family goal. Start small and work towards bigger goals, and your confidence will become stronger and stronger. We are training our self-confidence, and we are retraining the way your mind thinks.

11. Write Your Autobiography

Before you tell me your life isn't interesting enough, let me promise you that as a writer and a ghostwriter, every time people find out what I do for a living they tell me about a project they are writing. The number of people with horribly boring lives who are writing biographies and autobiographies tells me it doesn't matter where you are in life – you are allowed to do it.

The purpose of this exercise is not to become a millionaire or the most famous writer in the world; it is to begin to treat your life as a success. When you're writing an autobiography, you focus on highlights in your life, and you start to remember and look at the things you've accomplished in your life. You don't believe in yourself because you have forgotten most of your great successes. It's time to stop underestimating yourself. Your journey might be inspiring for people.

When I first started writing books, my initial goal with my very first book I wrote was to sell ten copies. Just by having ten people buy my book and read my story, I would have affected the world. I achieved that first taste of significance. Once I had sold ten, I wanted to sell one hundred, and then one thousand. What matters is the first time you affect someone. The first time you get an email and someone says, "You changed my life," "You motivate me," "You give me hope again," "You got me excited about life." These words are the words you want to hear; they make you feel good, and they are my favorite words to hear. In fact, I look forward to you emailing me after you finish this book to tell me how you are beginning to fall in love with yourself all over again.

This is a very therapeutic and inspirational process that will help you connect with yourself. Writing your story is exciting, and yes, I will read it. I will be the first person to check it out and give you that first review. I'm happy to do it.

12. Read Inspirational Biographies

Find stories from real life that you can connect with and that motivate and inspire you. One of the books I most remember is the 800-page biography of General George Patton. One of the most amazing books I have ever read, and I read a new book every day!

When you read, and you know that the main character has a chance to fail, you know there's a possibility that things could go wrong; there are real stakes. That's what makes a book interesting for me: it feels real. If you choose a biography and know how it ends, the stakes are still real because in the moment, when things are happening, negative possibilities are a reality. My first successful book under own my name is called *Serve No Master*. It's the name of my brand, website, and most of my projects. It is an autobiography, and that's why people find it inspirational; it has a lot of ups and downs and failure and challenges.

If you want to read that book, you're more than welcome to, but the purpose of this book is not to get you to buy other books of mine.

Find stories that inspire you; find a real person to become your hero. I listen to a podcast with a television writer whose politics I am very much not in line with; many things he says and believes I totally disagree with, but I do like that is he is obsessed with Abraham Lincoln. It is his favorite president, and whether or not you agree with someone's ideas, I always like it when someone is passionate and very knowledgeable about something.

Find people in history that inspire you. I find Patton very inspiring, and I can tell you loads of stories about him. Patton was so good at winning that all the other generals were freaking out. The British were enraged because they wanted to be the ones to free Paris and Berlin and were in talks with Patton's superior. Patton was the number two in charge of the third army. They said, "You have got to stop this guy; he is winning too much." I would love if people said that about me! "Give everyone time to catch up; you are winning too much!"

They couldn't get him to stop. He kept saying, "I interpreted your orders to just take more territory, so I did. Forty-four cities in the last week. Apologies I can't slow down, caught in the heat of battle. Can't stop fighting, can't disengage, have to keep winning." He was an unbelievable general, but he also made lots of mistakes when they tried to make him a politician in North Africa. (Special note: I am currently writing a thriller with the daughter of one of Patton's tank drivers!)

Patton is a historical figure that inspires me. You have to find your hero. Patton isn't my only hero, he is by no means the only historical figure I like, but it's one that I enjoy reading and talking about. Find stories where there are real stakes, and you will feel the difference.

Reflection Questions

In your Love Yourself Journal, write down the answers to the following questions:

1. Which of the techniques from the previous section resonated with you? Which ones are you excited about trying and which ones are you already implementing in your life? Maybe you are already doing things and didn't realize how good they were for you.
2. Which new technique do you want to try first?
3. How much room for growth do you see in front of you in the area of intrapersonal skills?

Exercise

For the next two weeks, you're going to implement at least five of the techniques from this chapter. I recommend you wait on jumping to the next chapter until you work your way through this drill. You should have written down the techniques that you are going to try in your Love Yourself Journal, and you should give yourself a full for fourteen days to experience this process and then answer these questions:

1. Do you feel you have a greater sense of self-awareness?
2. Describe how your self-awareness has improved.
3. What could you have done better over the past two weeks?
4. What will you do in the future to ensure your self-awareness continues to grow and improve?
5. Do you feel like your ability to control your thought life is stronger?
6. How do you feel your thought life has improved or grown over the past two weeks?
7. How are you going continue to improve and grow in this area?
8. Do you feel you have a stronger ability to monitor and control your thinking? Explain why or why not? How do you plan to continue your development in this area?

3

THE MOUNTAIN OF WISDOM

"Wisdom" is a word that we sometimes use interchangeably with "smart," "intelligent" or "knowledgeable" but that is not what the word means. There are plenty of people who know a lot of stuff but demonstrate no wisdom. When I was younger, I always thought that older people had wisdom; I thought you automatically got wisdom with age. As I have aged, I have learned that there are plenty of people older than me who are foolish and make terrible decisions, and the last thing I want to do is take advice from them. I do not want my life to turn out like theirs.

There are so many people my age whose lives have gone in directions that I don't want my life to go into. When I look at all the people in my life who have given me advice, so many of them have missed the mark, and if I had taken their advice, my life would have turned out much worse. There were also some people whose advice was good, and I wish I had taken it. They had a bit of wisdom.

Let us think about our definition of wisdom, and what exactly the word means. Before we can achieve wisdom, we need to be sure of our definition. Let's start with a brainstorming exercise.

Brainstorming Exercise: Our Definition of Wisdom

Open your Love Yourself Journal. If you have the official Love Yourself Journal, you can see this section and work it out there; otherwise, you can use your own notebook and create a new section. I want you to write out your definition of wisdom. Give it a good paragraph. You can also describe a person who you think is wise.

Everyone has different answers and different definitions of wisdom. Allow me to try to capture my definition of wisdom so that you know exactly what I am trying to help you achieve. I think of wisdom as something similar to the term "street smarts." Street smarts means knowing how to make the right decisions in the right situations. We think of "book smarts" as the ability to solve math problems and to do good work in the classroom or office. Street smarts is knowing when to ask for a raise, or when to leave a room before a bar fight breaks out. It is about your decision-making process.

Wisdom is the ability to make the right choices when they come in front of you. That is my definition of wisdom, and that is what we are going to move towards together. As you begin to love yourself and develop charisma, you will come into alignment.

We often lack wisdom because our conscious and subconscious desires are not in alignment. We say we want to make more money, but we don't work hard, we think rich people are stupid, and the last thing we would ever do is take a night class. Your desire and actions are not in alignment. It is hard to achieve wisdom when the two parts in your mind are at war with each other.

Exercises

1. Everyone has areas of wisdom in their life – areas where they are an expert and make great decisions. In your Love Yourself Journal, write down an area you feel you have a great deal of wisdom, a good decision-making process, or a good deal of expertise, and you feel comfortable with that wisdom. Write down times where other people

have acknowledged this wisdom or asked you for guidance, advice, or knowledge.

2. Write a long entry about your hidden wisdom – something that you know a great deal about, but you don't like to talk about. Maybe you can understand the baseball card market or comic books, or perhaps you know a great deal about how they score boxing matches. Write down a little bit about an area of expertise you haven't shared with anyone yet, and why you have kept it to yourself.

4

WHO DO YOU LOVE?

You grabbed this book because you want to be someone who loves themself. But love means something a little bit different to each person. We have all seen people who are in very bad, abusive or unhealthy relationships, and yet they both say they love each other and treat each other completely differently. For some people, love means having a person that they can say horrible things to and have complete dominion over. That is certainly not my definition of love. We want to be very crystal clear on what it means to "love yourself."

I want to share with you my personal definition of what it means to love yourself and what you are going to achieve as you work your way through this book and the included exercises and activities.

1. Believe in yourself absolutely.

Many people are perfectionists; we hold ourselves to the highest standards, and we demand levels of ourselves that we would not demand of anyone else. When we fall short, we never forgive ourselves. We are often still reliving mistakes and dumb decisions we have made in the past, or areas where we have let ourselves down. This affects how we view ourselves.

If I were to ask you to rate yourself as a human, on a scale of one to ten, you are probably going to give yourself a three, five, or seven. These are the most common scores people give themselves. If you don't believe in yourself as a ten, no one else ever will. You are limiting your world, and this is a sign that you don't love yourself enough.

2. Recognize that you can't change the past.

It is very tempting to dwell on the past and look at the decisions that you made and the things you wish had gone differently. You might look at the times you missed great opportunities – jobs, friendship, or the girl or guy you let get away. I had many friendships and relationships when I was younger that are gone now, but I don't agonize over them. Friendships disappeared regularly before the advent of social media, while now people stay in your life forever, even if you don't want them to.

You have to accept that the past is written in stone and cannot be changed, and therefore worrying about it is a waste of time.

We want to invest time and energy in things that we have the ability to change. That means the present and the future. What you do in the "right now" is more important than anything else. If you have made mistakes in the past, it is time to forgive yourself and say, "I can't control or change the past; all I can control and affect is the present. That is where I am going to focus right now."

3. Accept yourself.

Everyone has flaws and areas of weakness. I am not perfect, and I accept that. I accept myself exactly how I am. Have you ever been in a relationship with someone and you realized they just wanted to change you – they saw you as a ball of clay they could mold into their dreams?

In my early twenties, I dated a girl who wanted to change everything about me. She wanted to change my career, my major in college, the type of music I listened to, the clothes that I wore, the city that I lived in, and my diet. When I said to her, "Why do you want to change me so much?" She started crying and said, "I don't want to change you, what are you talking about?"

Shockingly, this relationship did not work out. You don't want to be in this type of relationship with yourself either. If anyone should accept you, it's you. We all have flaws, we all have areas of weakness, just accept yourself and stop punishing yourself for not being "perfect."

4. Be on your own side.

When I was in high school, I had a good friend named Michael. I remember how we met, and I even remember what he was wearing the first time we met. There was a girl he was friends with that I really liked.

A few months later, after he introduced us, I ran into her in a restaurant, and she said, "You don't still hang out with Michael, do you?" She started badmouthing him, so I said to her, "He is my friend, and he always will be; he is a great guy." I missed the opportunity to make something happen with this girl because I stood up for my friend.

Shortly after that, Michael was in a car accident and passed away. When she showed up at his funeral, I wasn't really excited, but I was proud of myself because the last thing I did before he died was defend my friend.

You should be exactly the same way about yourself. Stand up for yourself. Sometimes people will disparage you and say unpleasant things that knock you down. In those moments, you can say, "You just don't understand that I am actually good at this. Just because you don't believe something, it doesn't matter. You can tell me the sky is brown; it does not mean I am going to believe you. You have your thoughts and opinions, and that is fine. You can have whatever you want, but I believe in myself; I am on my own team."

5. Take care of yourself.

Life is all about balance. Thomas Jefferson believed that we should enjoy all things in moderation. You need to take care of both the physical and the mental. You need to take care of your relationships with other people and, most importantly, your relationship with yourself.

Our lives can be divided into three categories: health, finance, and relationships. If you are good in two categories and the third one falters, then everything collapses. You can have all the money in the world, but if you become sick, then you have got a big problem that becomes your entire focus. Those other areas of strength no longer matter.

Finding that balance is very important in all areas. You should try to achieve balance spiritually and emotionally, making sure that your mental and physical health are all in alignment. You should take care of your body and show that you respect it. You should take care of your mind and show that you care about it. This does mean that you need to eat a little healthier.

When you eat unhealthily, it can affect your self-confidence and your stress levels. The thoughts we have are also caused by the chemicals in our brain, and if we have lots of bad chemicals in our bloodstream, it leads to more bad thoughts. There is an interrelationship between our body and our mind; take care of both, and both will become stronger.

6. Acknowledge how amazing you are.

Nine people saw this book and did not buy it before you did; you made a decision to improve your relationship with yourself that at least nine other people didn't. Out of the next ten people that bought this book, nine didn't get this far; most people don't finish the books they buy. We buy books, we read part of them, and then we stop, especially with nonfiction. I am guilty of this just like everyone else. Because you have made it this far, you are starting to separate yourself from the crowd. You should be proud of yourself! You are showing that you are an amazing person who is dedicated to improving their life, and you should never forget that.

7. Don't be overly critical of your looks.

This is an area where a lot of people get caught up. Sometimes, people will take the time to let me know that I am ugly. I have gotten emails, and I have had people tell me in person. I have been told that my face is ugly, that I am fat, that I am gross. Guess what? None of that matters; those people don't matter. The only thing that matters is what you believe about yourself.

A few years ago, when I was about thirty years old, I joined eHarmony. I was curious about the site. It recommended to me only women that were all at least fifteen years older and fifty to a hundred pounds heavier than me. That did not make me feel good. It turned out that eHarmony was dead wrong. My wife is half my weight and a little more than half my age, and she thinks I am a really good-looking guy. That is all that matters; you only need to find one person out there who thinks that you are good-looking.

It is very easy to get caught up in what you think your flaws are. They interview Victoria's Secret models all the time and ask, "What is your least favorite body part?" And they'll say, "Oh, I hate my ankles. I hate this side of my butt. I hate this ear." Everyone has something about themselves that is not perfect, or that they are not happy with. But if that's all we focus on, it's a waste of energy.

8. Bring out the best in yourself.

You don't always have to win, but you have to do your best. I have made many mistakes in business, life, and relationships. I have invested in a huge amount of projects that have failed. I have been in situations where things got so stressful that there was talk of suing each other, but when we went over the list of the work I had put in, they said: "Ok, you have given your best; it is not your fault that this project has failed."

That is what people are looking for: a demonstration of effort and belief. As long as you do your best, you cannot ask yourself for anything more. Your best won't always be good enough – you can't always be perfect at everything. But as long as you keep doing your best, you will continue to grow as a person and can be proud of the effort you put in.

9. Don't let other people bring you down.

Your life is a movie, and you are the star of it. Everyone else around you is an "extra" in the movie of your life, and they don't even get speaking parts unless you allow them to. When I was in college, I was in love with a deaf girl, and I had a lot of deaf friends. If one of them did not like something someone was saying, they would simply close their eyes.

Closing their eyes was the ultimate unacknowledgement of the other person; it was a way of saying, "I don't care what you have to say; I am blocking it out." They would easily take away someone's speaking part if they wanted to.

We all possess this power. What other people have to say doesn't matter unless you let it. If people have negative thoughts or hostile attitudes, just ignore them. Cut them out of your life and forget it; they don't matter. They are not the star of the movie; you are.

10. Experiences are opportunities to grow.

Whether good or bad, whether you succeed or fail, every new experience is an opportunity for you to learn and grow as a person. Those though things from your past did not weaken you – they made you stronger. We learn more from our mistakes than from our successes, so a few failures along the way are okay. If you see your past as a series of events that brought you to this amazing moment right now, you can be excited about that. If your past had been a little bit different, you might not even be reading this book. I am glad your past has brought you to this point.

Reflection Questions

Look through the list of ten things we have just discussed. Which of these ten are areas where you are already strong and which do you see as areas of weakness for you? Where do you still struggle? Do other people's words hold you back? Do you feel sometimes you are holding yourself back with mistakes that you have made in the past?

The more you understand yourself, the more you work your way through these assessments, the quicker you will find the light at the end of the tunnel. Analyzing and finding the areas where you are stronger and weaker will help you to know where to focus your next round of efforts.

Introduction to Self-Esteem

Self-esteem is another word we hear being used all the time. We often hear it mixed up with self-confidence, but they are not the same thing. Self-confidence is how much you believe in your ability to do something and accomplish things. Self-esteem is how you measure yourself as a person. Remember when I asked you to assess yourself on a scale of one to ten as a person? That was a little top-secret self-esteem test.

5

SELF-ESTEEM ENGINE

In case you missed it at the end of the last chapter, self-esteem is your mental and emotional concept of your worth and value as a person. It is how much you think you would pay for yourself. It is more powerful than just how you feel inside; it affects your entire life. Your self-esteem will affect how you approach decision-making, the goals you will pursue, and what opportunities you consider as possibilities. It is nearly impossible for me to tell you how important self-esteem is. It's the lynchpin of the entire process of falling in love with yourself, developing powerful charisma, and creating the life you have always dreamed of.

If you have low self-esteem, when people bring opportunities to you, you will turn them down because you think you will fail. Someone walks up to you and says, "Hey, we would like to hire you for this project; we are going to pay you double what you make in your current job." You turn the job down because you think that you will try the job, fail, and end up unemployed and back at zero.

Case Studies

Let me give you a few examples to take this a little further. Take some time to read each of these examples and reflect on them. After each of these case studies, there are going to be a few reflection questions that I would like you to fill out in your Love Yourself Journal.

CASE 1: Mary is a very smart girl, and she will be entering her final year of high school this coming September. Despite her definite intellectual potential, Mary has very low self-esteem. She thinks that she is of average intelligence, and while her friends dream of becoming doctors or lawyers, she thinks she will be lucky if she just finds a steady office job. Because of how her low self-esteem is affecting her thinking, she has chosen to take courses in her final year of high school that will limit her ability to apply to good colleges or universities.

Question: How will Mary's low self-esteem affect her life, in both the short and long-term?

CASE 2: James is a college student. He has a strong desire to contribute to his campus and help his fellow students, and he has lots of innovative and exciting ideas. However, his low self-esteem is leading him to believe that he has nothing much to give and that the members of the student council are more intelligent and innovative than he is. He does not run for student council.

Question: How will James' low self-esteem affect his life in college? How might it affect his life long-term, as a result of the decision it pushed him to make?

CASE 3: Meredith is extremely hard-working and dedicated. In fact, she is probably the most hard-working and dedicated employee in her office. However, she has low self-esteem and constantly underestimates her abilities and the contribution she makes to her workplace. As a result of this, she has not pursued a promotion, even though many other much less worthy co-workers are clamoring for one, only too happy to be rid of the competition.

Question: How will Meredith's low self-esteem affect her career prospects?

What is the State of Your Self-Esteem?

Now reflect on yourself. What is the current status of your self-esteem? What do you think is the current level of your self-esteem? How would you rate your self-esteem?

It's very hard for us to accurately measure our self-esteem because we are so used to seeing things the way we do we are not able to be objective anymore. We're going to have to put in a little work together to achieve that. We often see aspects of ourselves and aspects of our self-esteem as natural – just as a part of who we are.

If you have had self-esteem problems for a long time, you might even think that you're a realist, not a pessimist, "I don't have low self-esteem. I just realized what I am actually worth; I am just assessing myself. My belief that I would fail this job is accurate." We become so ingrained in those beliefs that we limit ourselves, and we are blind how much low self-esteem is hurting and damaging us.

This is dangerous because self-esteem affects all the important decisions in our life, and it it's low it can become a self-fulfilling prophecy. We turn down great opportunities because we don't think we will succeed; we don't believe in ourselves. Later on, when life hasn't gone the way we thought it should, we forget all of those opportunities we turned down, and we look back and go, " I was always right; my life never turned out well as I didn't think it would. I was right from the beginning." We feel a justification even though it's a justification for unhappiness.

Self-Esteem in 3D

Below is a list of self-esteem questions for you to answer with a "yes" or "no." We are going to use these to measure your self-esteem and get a 3D picture.

When I was a volunteer on an ambulance, I learned how to attach the leads to the heart monitor. The basic setup is four stickers. You can put one on each wrist and ankle, and you get a decent two-dimensional view of the heart. For a more serious patient, someone having a heart attack or in a serious situation, we need to go 3D; we need the best image possible, and in that case, we connected twelve leads. We would start with the four basic ones and then do a series across the chest, to look at the heart from every possible angle.

That is why here we have quite a few questions to dig deeper here. Answer each of them with just "yes" or "no."

1. Do you tend to feel inadequate compared to others?
2. Are you very hard on yourself when you make a mistake or fail at something?
3. Do you find yourself always taking the position of follower rather than leader?
4. Do you find it difficult to assert yourself?
5. Do you feel a sense of dislike towards yourself?
6. Do you generally lack self-confidence?
7. Do you doubt that you deserve happiness?
8. Could the negative feelings you have about yourself make you less likely to try new things and put forward your talents?
9. Do you tend to assume people don't like you or look down on you?
10. Do you generally feel too intimidated to express your opinions in front of others?

Add up your answers to the questions above and give yourself one point for each answer. The more or points you have, the more work we have to do. If your "yes" answers are a full ten, we have a lot of ground to cover. If you just have one or two, we don't have as much work to do, but we still have to get it done.

Take a moment to reflect on your results. Are you surprised by how you answered some of these questions? Are you surprised to find that your self-esteem wasn't where you thought it would be?

If you are starting to panic, don't worry; you are just becoming aware of some of the flaws in your self-esteem, and it will be much easier to correct them. You are on the path to success. As long as you continue working your way through this book, some amazing things will happen. Take a moment to write in your Love Yourself Journal how you feel about these results and anything else you noticed as you went through this exercise.

Reflection Questions

Write down in your Journal your answers to the following reflection questions.

1. Were you surprised by how many "yes" answers you gave in the quiz? If so, why? What surprised you about your answers?
2. Reflect on each question where your answer was a yes. Why was it a yes? What is holding you back in this area? What is causing this particular self-esteem hole?
3. Start to think about ways you can repair this damage. Are there tendencies you were already aware of, or have you noticed things you have never thought about before?

6

UNSTOPPABLE CONFIDENCE

Confidence is another word we use all the time without a clear definition. We are used to hearing, "He doesn't have enough confidence. He has too much confidence. You need to work on your self-confidence." In reality, most of us don't even know what that means, because most people use their own interpretation of the word, rather than the definition you find in the dictionary. We need to create our own definition of confidence – something we can agree on so that you know what I mean when I talk about it.

I think of confidence as how much you believe in your ability. It is your self-assessment of your ability to handle a situation. You can be confident in one area, but not in another. You may be very confident in the boardroom, but the thought of talking to an attractive man or woman at a bar gets your knees shaking; it's overwhelming.

For some of us, our struggle is with our overall sense of confidence; we don't think we are very effective as a person. When you have very low self-confidence, it starts to reveal itself in other aspects of our personality. We start to show off depression, we hesitate to take opportunities, and we miss chances that come our way. A lack of confidence is often the reason why we miss some of the greatest opportunities in life because we simply think that we don't have what it takes; we don't believe that we would succeed.

Reflection Questions

In your Love Yourself Journal, write down the answer to this question: How self-confident are you?

It is always fascinating to me when I ask people this question. The way they answer is almost as important as the answer itself. Some people give themselves a score on a scale of one to ten. People with low self-confidence say three; people with high self-confidence say seven. No one wants to say ten because that feels pretentious, even though a ten on the self-confidence scale is really what we are striving for. It is what you should have.

How much you believe in yourself and how you talk about the way you believe in yourself is very important. The language we use reveals a lot about our internal thinking. Some people describe confidence only in relation to other people, "I am confident but I am not as confident as Tim." Take a few moments, write a couple of paragraphs, and spend some time getting to know yourself.

Components of Self-Confidence

Self-confidence has several other components. It includes self-esteem, which is how much you like yourself or how much you think you are a good or worthy person, but it also includes self-efficacy. As you can probably guess, self-efficacy is a measurement of how effective you think you are. A classic example of this that I think you can relate to is driving. The first time you sit behind the wheel of a car, there is no confidence in your ability to drive. You have no belief in your efficacy because you don't know how to do it.

You may believe and have self-esteem that you can learn to drive and that you have the ability to drive within you, but you certainly don't believe you can get in the car, turn the key, and drive without anyone teaching you. If you already know how to drive, you have a complete and total belief in your efficacy. You believe that you know how to drive because experience has led to belief and confidence.

Before you jump to the next section, take a few moments, to reflect on these questions: do you believe in yourself? Do you like yourself? Do you believe you are effective? Do you believe you are someone who is capable of completing tasks? Are there any tasks that I could put in front of you right now that you would be completely and utterly incapable of completing? Or given enough time, do you believe that you could conquer any challenge or puzzle?

Confidence Test

Below is a test that will help give you an idea of where your confidence level is at this point in time.

1. How willing are you to stand up for your opinion when it seems to go against everyone else's?
   a) Quite willing or very willing.
   b) Not very willing or not willing.

2. How easily and freely do you admit to mistakes you've made?
   a) Quite easily and freely or very easily and freely., and then I move on to learning from them.
   b) Not very easily or freely, or with great difficulty. I often go to great lengths to hide my mistakes.

3. How much are you governed by what other people think or might think?
   a) Not very much at all or not at all.
   b) Quite a bit or a lot.

4. Are you willing to go outside of your comfort zone in order to accomplish something?

    a) Yes, I usually or always am.

    b) Not usually or never. I'm too afraid of failure.

5. How positive do you feel about your abilities?

    a) Positive or very positive.

    b) Not very positive or negative.

6. How do you tend to mentally respond to real challenges?

    a) With excitement!

    b) With apprehension. I'm afraid of "showing myself up," so to speak.

SCORING: THE MORE "A" answers you chose, the stronger your confidence level is. If you chose a lot of "b" answers, you have a bit of work to do on boosting your level of self-confidence.

Self-Observation Exercise

For just one day, keep your Love Yourself Journal handy, or if that is too inconvenient, keep your phone nearby, and every time you notice yourself doing or saying something that demonstrates low self-confidence, make a note of it. If you aren't sure what these instances are, you can look at the previous test and add any "b" answer as a low self-confidence answer.

Take a look at your behavior throughout the day. You may be doing little "no-self-confidence" things that you aren't even noticing, and that is what we want to start to catch. We want to spend one day being focused on who you are, what you are accomplishing, and how you experience life. Maybe you notice an attractive man or woman, and you don't say anything. Maybe you are in an elevator with two people at work who are having a conversation that you want to jump into, but you don't. Maybe someone takes credit for your work, and you don't say anything. You go to the gym, and you have to choose whether to go to the beginner or the advanced class, and you choose the beginner class even though you could probably handle the advanced class. Every time you do something like this, just make a note of it. We are trying to capture a baseline to figure out where you are right now.

I am currently going through a very similar experience. Last week, I bought a fitness watch. This watch tracks everything I do. It tracks every step I take, every time I go up a staircase, my heartbeat 24/7 – everything I do, it is constantly observing me. At first, I didn't change my behavior; I wanted to get a feel for where I was so that I could notice my improvements. I established a baseline before I started altering my behavior.

I've been pacing up and down my dock dictating this chapter all day. Right now, my watch is telling me that I have walked three kilometers today. I have taken over two thousand steps today, but I still need to walk five thousand two hundred and ninety-six steps to reach my daily goal.

Knowing my baseline, I can then see how I am improving. I can see how much exercise keeps me at the same weight and how much I need to do to get to the next level. We want to get a baseline for your confidence in the same way. As with certain actions I can improve the health of my body, we can do the same thing and use certain actions to improve the health of your mind.

At the end of your day tracking your self-confidence, transfer all your records to your Love Yourself Journal and analyze how you felt during the day. Then answer the following questions.

What areas of low self-confidence did you notice that you didn't realize you were struggling with? What do you feel were the causes of these areas of low self-confidence?

You may discover that every time you have a low self-confidence moment, it is because there is an attractive person in the room, or because there is a person of authority, or maybe it only happens in social situation but not business situations. This type of data can help you to laser target your efforts to improve your confidence and do better in the future.

Observation of Others Exercise

For the rest of the week, watch how the people around you behave. Keep your eyes peeled for signs of low self-confidence and other behaviors that reveal their lack of self-confidence. We are so busy living as narcissists, totally obsessed with ourselves that we often don't notice how other people are living and experiencing life. I want you to change that. I want you to notice how the people around you change. You can look for things like people looking down instead of looking at each other in the eye, people hesitating to give answers, people sweating – all these little signs.

After your few days of observation, it is time to crack open your Love Yourself Journal again and write down what you have learned. If you can learn that other people are just as nervous as you are, that is a major revelation. That is big news!

7

THE CHARISMA FUEL

The most common piece of dating advice is, "There is nothing more attractive than confidence. If you want to find true love, you have to be confident." We know confidence is important. I heard this advice so many times when I was younger, and I always said to myself, "Well, that is great, but how do I become more confident? Is there a secret to becoming more confident? Is there a special technique? Is there something that I can do?"

In this chapter, we are going to bridge the gap between confidence and charisma. I am going to share with you some techniques that I developed with my blood, sweat, tears, and frustration that I've only shared with private coaching clients in the past. But I'm about to share them with you.

Experience Breeds Confidence

If you implement this section of the book, you will become a very confident person. I like to fight mental problems in the real world. I like to fight them where they are weak. The way to build your confidence is with your body in the real world. It is very easy.

There are several ways you can improve your confidence that we all know about: go to the gym, develop new skills, get stronger, faster, and smarter. Those things are cool, and they do help a little bit, but we all know people with amazing bodies who still lack confidence. Confidence comes from competence, which means knowing how to do something and knowing how to do it well. Doing something over and over again means you eventually get to the point where you are no longer nervous about it.

One of my friends was a soldier. One time, I asked him about talking to women. He was very nervous about the thought of talking to a woman in a bar. I said, "You just spent nine months at war. Are you nervous when you kick in a door, and there could be something horrible waiting on the other side, like a booby trap or someone with a gun?" He said, "Talking to women makes me far more nervous." And I said, "Well, objectively, talking to a woman is far safer than fighting in a war zone. Being a soldier is a very dangerous career."

From that moment, we realized his lack of confidence was not objective; it was *subjective*. It was not based on reality; it was based on his perception of reality. We dug a little deeper, and we discovered that he had practiced tens of thousands of times with his team, kicking in door after door, and he had done in the real world hundreds of times. He knew that his team was relying on him every time he did it. Experience leads to competence, which leads to confidence. So what we want to do is physically manifest confidence.

Territory-Based Confidence

The way to develop true confidence is to capture territory. The more territory you control, the more confident you are. Look at rich people; when they own a lot of land, they are more confident. We are going to do the exact same thing, but whether you own land or not is irrelevant. I want you to start with your bathroom. I want you to become a monster – someone who is obsessed with every square millimeter of your bathroom. You are going to clean your bathroom and put everything in its place. You are going to be strict because your bathroom is your territory, and anyone who indicts your territory has declared war on you. This mindset shift will change your life.

The first time you yell at someone for moving things around in your bathroom, you might feel weird, but the second and third time you start to feel something different; you will start to feel like a king. Whether you have roommates or a shared bathroom, here is what you say, "This bathroom is my territory, and it will be exactly the way I want it to be. If you want to make a mess in this bathroom, you have to kill me first, because I own this territory. I have claimed this territory, and you will respect this territory."

Expanding Territory

You are making a statement of intent; you are staking a claim on the universe, and you are changing the way you view the world around you. We live in a world adrift. Most of us do not own our homes. Most of us are not in power at work. Our boss could fire us on a whim or embezzle the money away, and the government closes the business. There are millions of ways you can lose your job tomorrow that are outside of your control.

We live in a world where very few of us have enough control over our lives or destinies, but it is time for you to take back control. When I was younger, I always hated to clean the bathroom against my will.

When I realized how powerful this technique could be, however, I became the bathroom cleaner. Every time I have a roommate, I negotiate. I say, "Are you willing to clean the toilet after I am sick?" They go, "Oh gross, no!" Then I go, "All right; I will be the all-time bathroom cleaner, but you have to do the dishes, cook and do the laundry." And they go, "Okay, fine." The reason I chose the bathroom is because it is so small it does not take that long to clean it. Even if your bathroom is disgusting, at max, you are going to spend an hour getting it shipshape.

Once you master the bathroom (this may take you a few days or few weeks, and that is absolutely fine), I want you to begin expanding your territory; it is time to annex your bedroom. When I was younger,

I was very messy. In high school, I never really cleaned my room. I depended on my parents to do it and – big surprise – that was the time in my life where I had the lowest confidence. I am now very strict about the cleanliness of my home.

Your bedroom should always be perfect. Whether you are single or married, whether you have roommates or not, none of that matters. It is about you taking control. Do not blame the other person; if they are a mess, that is a sign that they have no power. Every time you clean your roommate's mess up, you are not their slave; you are demonstrating that they are powerless and weak.

You say, "Your efforts to make this house messy will fail every single time. You can refuse to pick up your clothes. You can leave your stuff around. I will always clean it, and I will always have this room clean because this is my house. This is my territory, and you do not have the ability to influence this room anymore. You do not get to live in a messy house, no matter how much you want to." As much as they pretend that they have turned you into their house slave, they have given away all of their power to you. They have given away their confidence and their self-belief.

When people come to visit the house and say, "Wow, the house is so clean," your roommate very likely will say thank you and take the complement. I want you to think about that for a second; they have taken and stolen a compliment that was meant for you. Why? Because they do not want to admit reality. They do not want to say, "I do not clean house. My roommate does, I am powerless." The one who cleans has the power.

You may go through a short period of doubt at this phase, wondering if I've somehow tricked you. Just stay the course. Within a few weeks, the power dynamic in your house will change. When people walk into a clean house and then see that your roommate's room is disgusting, they will change perspective. You are cleaning for a reason and keep that as your primary focus during this exercise.

As you take over your bedroom, you will then take over your living room, and then take over the hall. Eventually, your entire home becomes your territory. When your house looks amazing, you will start to feel amazing.

I remember a Latin aphorism that I learned in high school, "A sound mind in a sound body." It is very hard for me to be focused on work when my room is messy and disorganized. When your house is messy, it can be distracting. If you are single and meet someone amazing, and they want to go back to your house and your thought is, "My house is messy," you won't bring them home because you are ashamed, and you have lost an opportunity. You might very well have lost your chance with the one because you are not in control of your life.

As you take over more territory, your competence will change dramatically. This section is not about going to war with your room-mate. This is just an example of how powerful you can become in relation to anyone else living in your house. Whether it is your spouse, your kids, your parents, or your in-laws, it does not matter.

Take Over the World

Once you have complete and total dominion in your house, you can move on to your car. When I was in high school, I went to school with some very rich kids – we're talking sixteen-year-olds whose parents bought them Hummers and Ferraris. Those kids had no respect for their cars; they had no appreciation.

I also went to school with a poor kid who worked all summer for three years in a row to buy a broken-down car; it was the best he could afford, and he washed his car every day. He would stand in front of the house, take his shirt off, and wash his car like in a 1980s heavy metal video. Not because his car was expensive, not because his car was beautiful, but because his car was an expression of his dominion over a piece of the world.

You should treat your car the same way. I do not care if your car is a piece of crap; stop calling it that. I do not care if your car cost a hundred thousand dollars or fifty dollars. It does not matter. It is yours, and you have to treat it as part of your territory.

As you take dominion over your car, you learn how to fix the tires and change the oil, you get rid of those fast-food wrappers, and you start to feel different. When people see your car and go, "Is this brand-new?" you will feel good. They are not complimenting your cleaning skills; they are complimenting your dominion skills. They are respecting your power and your authority.

The beautiful thing when you take control of your car is that you now you have mobile dominion; wherever the car goes, your confidence goes. You are beginning to teach yourself that confidence can travel with you. Confidence doesn't necessarily have to be something tied to a single location; we can move around with it. Even if you start at level zero, this technique will work for your confidence. If you start out with higher confidence, it may take you a couple of steps before you start to feel the effects. By the time you have finished this exercise, your confidence will be a rock-solid ten; you will be fearless.

After you take dominion over your car, it is time to start using remote locations. How about your cubicle at work? It should be clean. It should be flawless. You do not need to wait for the janitor clean your desk. Are you five? Are you a teenager? Are you me at sixteen? No. You can and should take complete control of your universe. Your workspace is part of your world.

When your boss comes to your office and makes a mess, you say, "What do you think you are doing? You are my boss, and I will do any work you give me, but please do not make a mess in my workspace. This is my space, and I care about." If your boss says, "I do not like your attitude, you are fired," you can take it to court, and you will win every time.

When your boss says, "I fired him because he wanted his office too clean," he will lose ten times out of ten, and you can live off your winnings. No one can fire you for being a good steward. No one can say, "He took too good care of his desk; he cared too much about company property." If your boss goes to HR with this complaint, you'll have his job next week because every company wants a steward.

I know this is a slightly extreme example, but this is how important your territory should be. No one should invade once you have staked your claim.

There is nothing better than people who take ownership of their workspace and have confidence in their work. Take over more and more territory at your office until you feel comfortable and competent, and then you can also start with remote locations.

I talk extensively in my books on networking about how to take control of a venue like a bar or restaurant, and how to become someone who is dominant in this public and highly social locations. A friend of mine used to clean up glasses at his favorite bar; he would pick up all the glasses from messy tables after people had not put them on the bar, and people would ask, "Do you work here?" And he would go, "No, I just like being somewhere nice."

I like that. He is bending reality. He was not dressed like a worker, and people did not think he was a bartender; they thought was the owner or manager. Eighteen years old, cleaning up glasses because he took pride in the location and wanted the place to look nice, and people thought he was far more powerful than he was. He was projecting an unbelievable level of confidence.

The more territory you take over and the more you focus on it with the mindset of taking over territory, the stronger your confidence will become. What is cool about this technique is you do not even have to think about confidence; it is as a side effect. You will be so busy taking over territory and being awesome that the secondary effect is massive confidence spike.

Facets of Charisma

There are ten other facets of charisma. Think about how each of them applies to your life, and how much or little you have of each of these.

1. Energy. As humans, our energy levels rise or lower based on those around us. You know the saying, "Misery loves company." When

someone is very low in energy and enters the room, the rest of the room's energy drops.

As humans, our emotions equalize. If you are in the room with someone very energetic, they pull the energy up. Think about the guy you call "the life of the party." That's the person you want to bring to every party to make sure everyone is having a good time. They have high energy, they pull everyone's energy up, and they pull people's happiness up. This is a key facet of charisma.

2. Optimism – the belief that good things can happen; seeing the best in other people, seeing the best in the world, and seeing that things are getting better. I have friends who always talk about how everything is going to hell in a handbasket. They always talk about politics and the government. They always talk about how the dollar is going to collapse, the world is going to war, and the illuminati are going to kill everyone. I hate being around them. They suck the joy out of me; who wants to be around that?

Optimistic people, and even people that are almost too optimistic, are great to be around. You say to yourself, "Wow, this person is so happy; ignorance really is bliss." I would rather not know about anything in the newspaper; there is never good news in there. Optimistic people are very charismatic.

3. Enthusiasm – the excitement to do things. Here's a simple example. You have to go on a trip for work, and you have to take one person, either Tom or Susie. You say, "Hey Tom, we are going to go on a business trip this weekend" He goes, "Ah man, are you kidding me? I do not want to work on the weekends; are you going to pay me overtime? What if I have plans?"

Then you say the same thing to Susie, and she goes, "Oh my gosh, please take me! I am so excited! I love traveling, and I have the best new traveling mix CD. I cannot wait to get on the road with you." A part of you might think you do not want to listen to

Susie's road mix CD, and I totally get that, but at least she is enthusiastic.

You would much rather be around the person who is excited to go and feels positive about it. Enthusiasm is just a combination of optimism and energy.

4. Engagement. Some people are very reserved; they do not like to talk, and they keep their thoughts in. This is the opposite of charisma. Charisma is about pushing your energy into the world, and the only way to put your energy into the world is to actually interact with the world.

I am naturally very introverted, and this is why I avoid talking to other people on my island. You would not know that though, because anytime you would meet me would be at a conference. When I am out networking for my business, I activate the engaging part of my personality.

I spend three months talking to no one, and in three days I am talking to everyone 24/7. I turn my energy levels off until I need them. You can do the same thing.

5. Intelligence. It is not just about being smart; it is about demonstrating your intelligence. There are different types of intelligence. I have friends who do not know how to read, but if we are in the woods, they know how to survive under any circumstance. The idea that IQ is the be-all and end-all of intelligence is ridiculous. It does not matter in what area your intelligence is; it is about demonstrating it.

If you are very good at tying knots, let people know. It is engaging. People are attracted to expertise and passions. When you show them things you are good at and you know a lot about, they will be pulled into that.

I have a friend who can build an entire house on his own. Anyone who met this guy would think he's dumb because he is not book-smart at all. In most areas of intelligence, he is not very strong, but when he gets inside that house and picks up a drill, he is unbelievable. When he is building and working non-stop, he is very charismatic. I like watching him work. I tried to help him once, but I am so terrible with tools that I am not allowed to anymore.

6. Be interesting. How tough is this? It is like walking up to a comedian and saying, "Hey, be funny."

Here is how to become more interesting: do what you want. Stop doing what other people want you to do and start doing whatever you want to do. If you are sixty-seven and want to get good at ice skating, do it. It is way more interesting than just watching television.

When I was in high school, I thought that I needed to watch every single television show so I could talk to people about whatever they were watching. I wanted to be connected to what I called "culture." I wanted to be able to jump into the conversation every time people were talking about a show. For a long time, I was able to do this, but I had only surface relationships; I had no actual friends and no actual conversations. I was uninteresting.

When you start to cultivate exceptional hobbies, which are the things that are different than other people's usual activities, that is when you become interesting. On the other hand, striving for popularity and to be just like everyone else is the biggest mistake you can make because it makes you boring. You become a two-dimensional character and fall into a stereotype.

So many people want to be against mainstream culture and say, "I am different to everyone else!" And they are standing with twenty people wearing the same clothes, listening to the same bands, and doing the same things. In order to be interesting, you have to do interesting things, and there is always something special within you that you want to do. Maybe you have not done it yet because you thought, "It is too simple, it is not cool, it is not popular." You should do it anyway, whatever it is, because doing what you like is going to help you become more charismatic.

7. Be assertive. When you meet other people, they are going to push back against you to see how strong your sense of self is. When I was a single guy, girls were always asking questions to see if they could make me doubt myself. Not because they were monsters, but because they were testing me to see if I was self-confident. A lot of people can project a pseudo self-confidence that is not real. Sometimes people are going to say things to you that are mean or tough to see if you push back. They want to see if you have got some backbone, and it is far better to die on your feet than to live on your knees. No one will ever follow someone who is non-assertive, and you know that.

8. Good interpersonal skills. Charismatic people are very good at communicating with other people. I cover advanced interpersonal skills in this book and in many other books in this series because it's a crucial element. You can get good at communicating with people. One of the easiest ways to do it is by asking questions about them and actually care, which leads us to number nine.

9. Show interest in other people. They used to say that Bill Clinton made you feel like you're the only person in the room; he made you feel like an important person in the room, and the guy was the President. Whenever the President is in the room with someone else, the other person usually does not matter. The President is always more important. Yet, he got there by making other people feel important. He was able to project this amazing ability, and it led him all the way to the White House two times in a row.

Faking interest in other people is very hard. It is far better to actually master it. Find a way to be interested in other people. Every time I meet a new person, I ask what their job is. I want to meet one person from every possible job, and this helps me to become interested in other people and therefore very charismatic.

10. True leadership. Leadership is not easy. Most people think of leadership as telling other people what to do. True leadership is suffering when your team suffers. A true leader will send his soldiers to die and have nightmares for the rest of his life; that's leadership. A true leader would work extra hours and put in extra time so that his team does not have to get downsized. He will fight for his team; that is leadership. Leadership is not about sitting on a throne; it is about the weight of the crown on your head. Heavy is the head that bears the crown. When you lead through sacrifice, rather than through avarice, that is when you are a true leader, and people will strive to follow you.

Reflection Questions

Answer these questions in your Love Yourself Journal.

1. Has anyone ever called you charismatic or said that you are a natural leader? How did it feel? What were you doing at the time? What aspect of your personality were they responding to?
2. How charismatic are you on a scale of one to ten? If you were a video game character, how many points would you give yourself for charisma? What do you think you could do right now to raise your charisma level?
3. Now think of your charisma avatar. This is one person you have met in real life who is very charismatic. Describe them in great detail. My charisma avatar was a guy called Nathan. I met him in high school, and I studied the way he treated people. He taught me how to be popular. I mimicked him and became like him because he was a good person, and he made me a better person.
4. Think about several charismatic people, whether they are people you know in real life, have seen on television, or

even read about in books. Look at what traits they have in common. Are there traits from the list that they share with you? Is there something else that I have not covered yet?

5. How do you feel a higher level of charisma would change your life? Would it improve your dating life, your business life, your friendships? Would it improve your happiness? How will your life be different when you come out the other side and you are more charismatic?

8

THE TRIAD OF SUCCESS

We often think of charisma as an unmeasurable force or an unknown quality that people have or don't have from birth. It is something we can't look directly at; we can only measure its effects. We can't tell if someone has charisma when they are in isolation. Take a charismatic person, put them in a locked empty room, and you can't measure their charisma. You can only see when you get other people in that room how that person's charisma influences them.

When we struggle with popularity, charisma, and leadership, we think of it as this missing essence that we either have or don't have; there is nothing we can do about it because it is hard to measure it within ourselves. I can't determine how charismatic I am without talking to anyone else, without interacting with other people and seeing how they react. It is hard to figure out how we can improve.

We do know that self-esteem and confidence are core components of charismatic people. People who exude confidence, positive energy and belief in themselves draw people to them. The more you believe in yourself, the more other people believe in you. Look at leaders throughout history – even misguided leaders. They had a powerful force because they believed in themselves so much that even when they were wrong, people followed them. That is the power of their charisma and self-belief.

Before you can build up confidence in your ability to do things, you have to build up your belief in yourself, your self-esteem, and how much you like yourself. It is hard to push yourself for greatness when you don't like yourself, when you don't believe in yourself, and when you don't think that you are good enough.

Things to Think About

1. Think about the most charismatic people you know; it can be people in your life or people on television. You can look at great leaders throughout history. I used to know someone in college who loved to listen to great speeches from history. He thought if that he listened to enough speeches by charismatic leaders, it would eventually turn him charismatic. It did not work.

Take a look at some of the most charismatic people in your life and from history and then assess their confidence. Do you notice something in common? When you look at specific examples, you will start to see how there is a strong correlation between confidence and charisma in people. Not every competent person becomes charismatic, but every charismatic person certainly has a great deal of confidence that they project in the world.

Are you beginning to see the link between confidence and charisma? If you think I am dead wrong, that is okay; write that down in your Love Yourself Journal. It is okay to disagree with me and to begin to push yourself and start thinking about these ideas. This is all about helping your thought process evolve.

2. Take some time to reflect on the reasons for the link between confidence and charisma. Why do you think confidence helps us seem more charismatic to other people? When you think of someone you know in your actual life who is charismatic, do you think their confidence is what pulled you into their orbit?

3. Now that you have been with me on this journey for a little bit, do you feel more comfortable and excited about this process? Do you have some specific action steps that you are planning to take to move you further along this process to become more charismatic? Perhaps you have already taken some of the steps.

4. Think back to a time when you met someone who had very low self-confidence, or maybe a moment where someone revealed a deep lack of self-confidence. Did you notice a corresponding lack of self-esteem? At the time, were you repulsed or repelled by the force of their low self-confidence? Now that you have a better understanding, do you understand why we pull away from people with low self-confidence? Do you think differently about the situation now than you did at the time?

Reflecting on the Past Exercise

We are now going to go through eight scenarios, and I want you to reflect on each of them. Think of a time when you experienced each scenario and write your answers in your Love Yourself Journal.

1. Think of a time when your lack of confidence blocked you from convincing other people to take action. Maybe you were just trying to convince your friend to see a certain movie with you but you weren't sure that the movie would be good, or you weren't sure that you were making the right choice, and rather than taking people to a move they might not like, you let someone else decide and saw a movie that you didn't like. Whatever your example is, write it down in your Love Yourself Journal.

2. Think of a time when your lack of confidence kept you from asserting yourself when you should have spoken up or taken action. Maybe you have one of those stories from high school which we all have, when people were picking on someone, and you wished you had said something to stop them.

3. Think of a time when your lack of self-confidence stopped you from pursuing a goal. Did you want to pursue athletics into college? Did you want to pursue an artistic career and didn't think you were good enough? Maybe you did not believe that you had what it takes to go to the next level.

4. Did your lack of confidence interfere with your education? I had a friend who was significantly smarter than me. He was a self-taught autodidact, played five instruments, and was offered a full scholarship to college but didn't go; he thought he was too dumb. He was convinced that he wasn't good enough and he froze his education. Do you have an experience like this in your own life?

5. How about a time when your lack of confidence interfered with your career? Maybe you didn't apply for a job you could have gotten, or you didn't ask your boss for the promotion or say, "You don't need to hire someone else; I can do it."

6. Can you think of a time you felt frustrated? A time where your charisma was trapped inside you, and you could not express yourself the way you wanted to. You couldn't put together the right words or emotions – you felt trapped in your head, and you could not communicate with the world in the way you wanted to. Your charisma couldn't escape.

7. How about a time when other people's perception of your low-level charisma held you back? Maybe you were in school on a speaking team, doing a group project, and you said, "Hey, let me be the speaker!" They said, "No, you just help prepare the slides; you don't know how to be a good speaker."

I ran for office when I was in high school. There were eight positions on the Student Senate for my class, and I put together an unbelievable proposal – an entire strategy for making the school better. I put together my idea for a program for donating school supplies and clothes to less advantaged kids. My school was a very wealthy school, and I saw all these people just throwing away their clothes, so I said, "What if we did something a little better?"

When I gave my talk like everyone else, all the students voted against me. They said, "You have great ideas, but you were not charismatic enough." They voted for the popular kids, and nothing changed. In fact, several of the kids who won the popularity contest came and asked me for my plans so they could implement my ideas, but they never did because ideas are not enough.

Implementation is everything. But I learned a lesson that day: believing in something wasn't enough; if I couldn't pull people into my charisma, then my idea would die on the vine. Has this ever happened to you?

8. Do you ever feel trapped in a cycle, going from low charisma to low self-esteem, to low confidence, and back and forth again? People don't listen to what you have to say. They say negative things about you, and they say that you are not a good leader. They might say you don't know how to handle yourself, so you feel bad and stop believing yourself.

Maybe have not always been in the cycle, but perhaps there has been a time in your life when you felt trapped in it. Analyze how you felt in that moment and how you feel looking back at that moment.

Confidence and Charisma Experiment Exercise

There is another charisma and confidence technique that I have not shared with you yet. This technique is very powerful; I have implemented it in the past, and it was for transformative for me. It works very well in complement with the territory-based confidence technique. Maybe you have heard this term before; it is called "fake it until you make it." Understanding how this process works is the key to its success.

In your Journal, create version 2.0 of yourself. If you have read one of my other books where you have done the process before, it may be time for you to do a 3.0 version. Describe a version of yourself that is fully charismatic and has super high levels of competence and self-esteem. Describe the person that you wish you were. Imagine you are six months in the future and describe yourself in great detail. Create a three-dimensional character in your mind and then write every detail down in your Love Yourself Journal. This version 2.0 is the ultimate in charisma and confidence – the person you wish you were.

Once you've created this character and have a firm feeling of what confidence looks like when applied to you, you have to spend the next week pretending to be this person. You are going to be an actor for seven days, pretending to be your 2.0 or 3.0. You are playing a role, so you constantly have to ask yourself, "What would 2.0 say or do?"

Spend a week seeing how this character acts. You may go through a phase where you go too far in the other direction, and I've done this myself. I emulated a specific super-confident version of myself that was too far and became a jerk, so I calibrated down the following week. That's okay. It's better to push too far and then bring it back a little bit rather than spend the rest of your life wondering if you added enough confidence.

Pretend to be this person for a week. Every time someone asks you a question, you say what your 2.0 would say. At the end of each day, when you get home, open your Love Yourself Journal and respond to the following questions:

1. Did people treat you differently, as if you were more charismatic? How did it feel acting like a different person throughout the day?

2. How much do you feel that your change in self-confidence affected your charisma? Did pretending to be more confident actually make you more charismatic? Can false confidence create charisma?

3. Now that you have gone through this exercise pretending to be more confident, do you actually feel more confident? Do you feel like you made actual permanent changes to your confidence and charisma levels?

4. Do you feel that this exercise has improved your self-esteem?

5. Will you continue this exercise for the long term? Do you feel this exercise can become a permanent part of your life?

If you spend enough time pretending to be a better version of yourself, you will become that person. This is a very powerful technique. It starts at the opposite end of the spectrum. This technique starts with your interactions with other people; it starts with the outermost shell of your personality.

When combined with our territory-based confidence technique, which starts at your core, the process is twice as fast. These techniques work very well in tandem. They are unbelievably powerful.

6. Are you going to stick with this technique and continue to use it? Do you like seeing how the benefits work? Would you like to be this person all the time without doing it on purpose?

7. If someone walked up to right now and said, "You read that amazing book. How can I become more charismatic?" What would you tell them to do? What action steps would you give to someone else who wants to become more charismatic?

9

CHARISMATIC MENTORS

L et's take a look at some famous people who had amazing
levels of charisma. We will talk about their lives and their
attributes, and think about who they were. Read the stories
and then answer the questions n your Journal. One of the lessons
that you will learn from this endeavor is that people with different
personalities and different kinds of dreams and ambitions can all be
charismatic.

Marilyn Monroe

Marilyn Monroe was an overwhelmingly famous and iconic Holly-
wood actress. She is probably one of the most famous people who
have ever lived.

She was born as Norma Jeane Mortensen in 1926, in Los Angeles.
She was also called Norma Jeane Baker during her childhood and
adolescence. Her mother was a negative cutter at one of the movie
studios. Monroe's biological father is unknown.

Her mother was schizophrenic, and Norma Jean grew up mostly
in foster homes and orphanages. Soon after, she became an actress,
and she was told to change her name to something more "interest-

ing." She decided to use her mother's maiden name Monroe, together with the first name Marilyn.

Marilyn Monroe went through many traumatic experiences in her difficult childhood, and they had an effect on her throughout her relatively short life (she died of a drug overdose in her 30s). However, she was very intelligent – a great deal more than people of the time gave her credit for. She was also unique and energetic, and had a magnetic personality. These qualities, together with her beautiful appearance, helped her secure an incredible level of fame. Monroe is recognized as one of the most charismatic people to have ever lived.

Reflection Questions on Marilyn Monroe

Are you surprised that Marilyn Monroe had such a difficult life? Do you think she might have been more successful if she had experienced less trauma? Or do you think she somehow harnessed the sadness she went through to contribute to who she became? Now that you have learned about Marilyn Monroe, have you gained greater admiration for her? Why or why not?

Winston Churchill

Winston Churchill is one of the most well-known and charismatic prime ministers Great Britain has ever had. While he was born into an aristocratic family, he never felt like he really had a place when he was a child. He had a speech impediment and experienced a lot of emotional insecurity.

Winston Churchill's charisma is considered to be one of the key factors that helped keep up the morale of the British people during World War II, and it is thought that this high level of morale was instrumental in Great Britain and its allies winning the war.

Reflection Questions on Winston Churchill

What are your general thoughts on Winston Churchill and his life? Do you think you would like to learn more about him? Do you think that Winston Churchill's childhood experiences somehow contributed to his charisma?

Mahatma Gandhi

Mahatma Gandhi was considered to be a mediocre student when he was a child. Despite that, he had a profound and expansive intellect. Even though he was born into one of India's privileged castes, he spent his life fighting for the rights of the poor and oppressed and for India's independence from Britain. His ability to lead was unparalleled.

Gandhi's level of devotion seemed almost unprecedented, and he was totally committed to living by his principles and ideals. To accomplish his goals, he let himself be in many extremely dangerous situations and constantly engaged in self-sacrifice.

Reflection Questions on Mahatma Gandhi

Mahatma Gandhi's charisma and ability to lead were tightly linked to his immense capacity for empathy and self-sacrifice. What do you think we can learn from his life?

Princess Diana

Princess Diana was arguably one of the most famous people ever to have lived, and chances are you have seen dozens or maybe even hundreds of images of her (depending on your age). When Lady Diana Spencer married into the British royal family, her charisma ensured that she immediately became by far its most popular member.

Later on in her short life (she died in a car accident in her 30s), she became extremely involved in several important movements, such as the fight against the use of land mines. One of the things that Princess Diana was most known for was her caring demeanor, but also her ability to captivate people simply with her manner.

Reflection Questions on Princess Diana

What do you already know about Princess Diana? What have you thought about her in the past? What do you think made her as charismatic as she was?

Charismatic People Exercise

For this exercise, you need to think of one other charismatic person. This can be a famous person, or it can be someone you know in your day-to-day life. If you choose to write on a famous person, maybe you could even glue in a picture of him or her to help inspire you.

1. Write a description of this person's personality. What is it about this person that makes you find them so charismatic?
2. Write on what you know about this person's life. Do you think there are elements of their life (past or present) that have helped them become a charismatic person, directly or indirectly?

10

TURBOCHARGE YOUR SELF-ESTEEM

Self-esteem is a core component in this process, and we often look at self-esteem as something that you have or don't have it. Sometimes it's hard to figure out a way to improve it or to see it as something that we can change. We often think of self-esteem as a measurement of ourselves, not something that we can influence or affect. In fact, it can be changed, and this is something we can work on together in this chapter. I am going to take you through a few specific steps that can help you boost your self-esteem very quickly.

Twelve Techniques

1. Become aware of your thought life. Pay attention to your beliefs and thoughts. In particular, take notice when you start to have negative thoughts, or when a little voice in the back of your head says you are not good enough to succeed. Before we can trigger change, we have to be aware of the problem. The first step on this path is to notice negative thoughts that come to your head and tell you bad things about yourself. I have these thoughts about myself all the time. Sometimes I make mistakes, or bad things happen, and sometimes the thoughts just come from nowhere.

Last night, when I was recording this chapter for the first time, the recorder didn't work. I had to redo this entire section a second time. It made me feel like a bit of a loser. I had that thought, "What kind of loser messes up a recording?" I write all my books by dictation because of problems with my eyes; I can't be on the computer as much as I used to. Having made hundreds and hundreds of recordings this year, this is the first time it happened, but I felt pretty bad about it. I could have let that thought influence me, and it could have shut me down, but instead, I noticed it. I said, "This is a negative thought. If I ignore it, it has no power." And I didn't think about until right now because I want to share with you.

Thoughts only have power if we give them power. Emotions only have power if we give them power. Emotions are just thoughts, and if we ignore them, they disappear. We can train ourselves to push them away with distraction and by focusing on positive things.

2. Don't put yourself down. So many people are taught to say things like, "I am my own toughest critic. I hold myself to a higher standard than I hold anyone else to." Stop doing that. It's ridiculous and unnecessary, and it damages you. When you think negative thoughts about yourself, when you hold yourself to a higher standard, when you always make it harder for yourself, you are just making life more difficult for no reason. There is no benefit to this behavior. No one ever says, "I held myself to a higher standard, and it led my life to this benefit; it helped me make more money; it helped me find better love; it helped me fix this problem." It never works. It is an empty statement with no benefit; cut that of your life. Don't think bad things about yourself.

You should be your biggest fan. If you don't believe in yourself, no one else is going to believe in you. If you are reading this book right now and thinking, "This might work for other people, but it won't work for me because..." stop that thought before you finish it – it's wrong! Every single person has a different "because" – because I am too old, because I am too young, because I am a man, because I am a woman, because I am too fat, because I am too skinny, because I am too tall, because I am too short. How can something not work for two opposite reasons? That's ridiculous. Shut down those negative thoughts; do not give them power and do not put yourself down.

3. Do not confuse feelings with facts. Thinking for a moment that I messed up the recording and therefore I am a loser does not make me a loser in the real world. They are two very different things. Reality and perception are not the same thing. Do not give power to negative thoughts. There is this trend in our society to act as if emotions are so powerful they can take over you. We are always looking for excuses when we do bad things. "I murdered her because I was angry." Anger doesn't have power; it's just an emotion.

Emotion is just another thought. Do not mix reality with fiction thoughts in your head. Thoughts are not reality, and they are not objective; they are subjective. They do not have power over you unless you decide to give it to them. You are standing in a restaurant, and the waiter is staring at you. Your first thought is, "This waiter hates me. Why is he staring me? He must think he is better than me. He is going to poison my food." Then waiter walks up and says, "I love your hair! Sorry for staring, I was thinking of getting a new haircut because I really like yours." What is reality? Your initial thought? No, your initial thought was dead wrong. Having a thought doesn't make it true.

4. Stop assuming the worst. When I was younger, I used to say, "I expect people to betray me so that when they do, I'm ready for it, and if they don't, I am pleasantly surprised." This was how I lived my life for a long time. Is it any surprise that I was lonely? When you expect the worst from people, that is what you get. Negative thoughts and beliefs can become self-fulfilling prophecies.

The more you expect the worst from the world, the less people want to be around you. If you have to go on a business trip this weekend, do you want to go with the guy who is expecting the worst or the guy who says, "This is a great opportunity; amazing things might just happen!"

Pessimism repels other people; it makes no one want to spend time around you, and it makes you not even want to spend time with yourself. When you expect the worst from other people, you become an introvert. You start to lock yourself away from the world, and then you suffer from greater and greater loneliness. This is a cycle that will destroy you. Stop expecting the worst and start realizing that amazing things can and will happen for you.

5. Do not dismiss your achievements. Give yourself credit for the accomplishments in your life. You have done great things in your life, and you should be proud of yourself. We often look at our lives, and we discount all the things that we have made happen. We go, "Oh yeah, I did that, but it's not that big of a deal." There is nothing worse than someone who can't take a compliment.

When I was single, long before I got married and had kids, one of the first things I would say to a woman on a date or when I first met her was a strong compliment to see how she would react. There are certain people who can't handle compliments, and this is because there is disparity between their self-esteem and reality. No matter how beautiful and wonderful a woman seems, if she can't take a compliment, that is a signal that she has low self-esteem.

When people have low self-esteem, they can't accept compliments, and when there is disparity between how the world sees them and how they see themselves, there are always problems. When I was younger, I dated a woman who cheated on every single person she ever had a relationship with. She was very attractive, with a great personality, but thought very little herself; her low self-esteem drove her to cheat over and over and over again. People with low self-esteem don't have enough control over their lives.

This is where you can start to take control; this is where you can change your patterns and stop looking for external affirmation. If you don't believe in yourself enough, you need other people to believe in you to keep you floating, and this leaves you in a constant battle between needing compliments to survive and getting so many comments that you have to reject them. You need to be at peace with who you are as a person and be proud of the things you have accomplished; don't discount them.

6. Encourage yourself. When other people don't believe in you, that is when you need to believe in yourself the most. The majority of success in my younger life came when people told me that I would not be able to do something. "Jonathan, you are not good enough to do this. Jonathan, you will never succeed at that." When people tell me I can't do something, when no one else believes in me, and it is just me against the world, that is when my greatest self comes forward because I believe in myself. I believe that I am capable of greatness, and I believe that you are capable of greatness too. Until you accept that, you will always be limited by your lack of belief. It is not your skills, your intelligence or your body that is limiting you; it is your belief system. When we don't believe in ourselves enough, we turn down amazing opportunities.

7. Forgive yourself. We have all done bad things in life. I have done things in life that are nothing less than horrible. I have said horrible things to other people. When I was eighteen and in my first serious relationship, when the girl told me that she loved me, I broke up with her. I could not handle it. I had so much hate for myself that it could not coexist with someone saying they loved me.

A year later, I had to come back and apologize to her in person, as in becoming a little bit healthier in my mental state, I realized that I broke up with her in a horrible way. When you don't like yourself, you can't be in relationship with someone who likes you. Those two feelings are constantly at war with each other.

As you raise your self-esteem, the quality of your relationships will go up. High self-esteem people date high self-esteem people. My wife believes in herself a great deal, and I have a great deal of self-esteem too. Unlike the low self-esteem girl I dated in my mid-twenties, I know that my wife will never cheat on me. She doesn't need external affirmation. She believes in herself. She is a very strong person who doesn't seek external affirmation because she never got it when she was younger; she had to become strong on her own.

When your self-esteem is strong, other people will gravitate towards you. If you have done bad things in the past that you regret, if you have had a bad relationship, if you have done someone badly, if you have made a mistake, if you went to the wrong college, if you screwed around in high school and did not get to go to college – whatever your past mistakes are, you have to let go of them now.

When we hold onto the past, the past holds onto us. We should not give the past any power because we cannot affect it. Don't waste your time thinking about things that you can't affect. It is a waste of your emotional energy, and all it does is suck the life out of you.

8. Break negative thought cycles. If you have a test coming up next week and you spend all week thinking about how you are going to fail, you begin to have dreams about failing, and the night of the test you will oversleep. You will show up for the test late and tired, and you will tank the test. You believed you were going to fail, and you found a way to make it happen.

Negative belief can affect the universe because it affects your behavior. The same thing happens in unhealthy relationships. You are convinced that the person you are with will eventually leave you, so you start to do things to drive them away. This is the plot of many Lifetime movies, so you probably know what I'm talking about. It is much easier to observe this process in other people than ourselves. The more power you give to negative thoughts, the more likely they are to influence you and affect your world.

9. Smell the roses. There is this belief in our culture that we have to suffer on the path to success, that the road to victory is paved in pain. In some areas, this is true. If you want to become a Special Forces soldier or a fireman, then yes, there's a lot of training, running, sweating, and lifting weights. But those are the exceptions, not the rule.

In most areas of life, we don't have to depend upon pain as the teacher. It is okay to enjoy the journey. You don't have to suffer along the way, and if you have a life where you aren't doing anything purely for pleasure, then this process will be very hard.

You need activities that you do for no other reason than they put a smile on your face. I have a lot of things that I love to do; painting, pastels, coloring books, playing the guitar, surfing, kayaking, and baseball batting cages. All of these things are fun for me, and none of them do I do for a specific purpose. They are not on the path to anything else. They are things I do simply to enjoy life. I love spending time with my children and swimming with them. This morning, I was in between two meetings on the phone, and I told the second meeting, "You are going to have to wait another thirty minutes. I am going to take my kids for a swim."

I have to enjoy the journey. I want to enjoy life. I don't want to sacrifice my youth so that I can enjoy my golden years. This is what corporations teach us in America as a way of controlling, manipulating, and forcing us to work jobs we hate, in hopes that someday, eventually, they let us have lives we are happy with. You can enjoy the journey along the way, so find things that you like to do. I recommend adult coloring books because they are easy, pleasurable, and very quick, and they are a path to becoming a great artist.

Art is a powerful therapy. This is why I design coloring books. It is an easy hobby. You can fit a pack of colored pencils and a coloring book in your briefcase; no one needs to know it is there. When you need ten minutes alone to chill out, you can pull it out. Find things you love doing and just do them!

I find things that are pure pleasure for me. I am thirty-six years old, married with two kids, and I still play video games. Not very often, but I do play a couple of hours a week. Whenever I start to feel little bit down, or a little bit weighed down by my work, I fire up the old video game system, and I play for an hour or two. It is okay to enjoy your life. Life does not have to be filled with suffering; it can be filled with pleasure.

10. Practice excellence. Doing things for pleasure is great, but there are also areas where you are excellent. Find things you are excellent at and do them more; confidence is built on a foundation of excellence. The more you know you are good at something, the more you have absolute confidence in this area.

I'm very good at driving. I've been driving for more than twenty years now, and I have passed driving tests on the left and the right side of the road. I can drive on either side, and I am confident about driving. Do I drive all the time anymore? No, but it is still something I am good at.

When you get good at something, that adds another brick in your wall of confidence, so do things you are good at. I don't just mean your work. You want to have hobbies that are outside of your work pattern that bring joy into your life. You may find you are very good things you never even considered.

You don't know what you're good at until you try it. One of the exercises I teach in my dating books, where I am teaching people how to become a better person, is to try a new hobby every week until you find what you are passionate about. Maybe it's going to be skydiving, maybe it's going to be photography, or maybe it is going to be running. Try lots of things, and you will find something you never realized you are naturally good at. The more excellence you have in your life, the easier it is to believe in yourself.

11. Practice mindfulness. I have already secretly taught you this, but maybe you don't know the term "mindfulness," or maybe you don't remember what it means. Mindfulness simply means living in the

moment. It means thinking about "right now." Not thinking about yesterday. Not thinking about tomorrow.

I could very easily be thinking about the lost recording from last night, wondering if I missed something I talked about last night, or if the previous recording was better than this one, and it could haunt me. I could also be thinking about when this book comes out; what if you don't like it? What if I get a bad review? That is the past and the future; thinking about those two things will only make this chapter worse.

Getting caught up in the past or the future is a waste of time. You cannot affect the past, and you cannot affect the future until it becomes the "now." This does not mean don't prepare for the future; it just means focus on what you are doing right now. The more you practice mindfulness, the more you find peace within yourself; the more you get caught in the moment, the easier it is to push away negative thoughts and build up your self-esteem.

One of the ways I build up my mindfulness is through sport. Every morning, my wife and I do Diamond Dallas Page yoga. He was a professional wrestler and now is a yoga teacher, and his DVDs are a blast. They are fun because he's got that wrestler's right-before-the-match excitement. We also did other types of meditative and peaceful yoga in the past, but I like his workouts. They are only twenty to thirty minutes, but they get my heart pumping. I feel good after I've done it, and when I'm doing the workout, I am so focused that I can't think about anything else. I can't think about the emails I want to answer. I can't think about the mistakes from last night. I have to live in the moment because what I'm doing is too hard.

It is the same when I'm surfing or paddle boarding or kayaking. When I am pushing myself, I don't have time to think about other things. This is why I have mentioned bringing sport and hobbies into your life. In my book *Coloring Away Depression*, I talk about coloring books as a way to cure away depression. If you fill your mind with something that takes up all of your attention, you have no time for negative thoughts. Coloring books are a powerful mindfulness tool.

12. Focus on the positive. Don't waste your time thinking about negative thoughts, mistakes, and problems from the past or in the future. All that stuff is a waste. No one wants to be around someone who is a glass half empty kind of person. I never spend time around negative people; I would rather be around positive people that pull my energy up and make me the type of person I want to be.

I want to be a positive person all the time. The more time I spend with positive people, the more my personality becomes positive. My wife is a very positive person; it is one of her greatest traits. She is always happy. She has a very casual approach to life. She is not worried about things all the time, and I love being around that; it makes life easier for me. When I'm around people that are negative or worrying all the time, it sucks the energy out of me.

Remember: between humans, energy equalizes. If you are near someone who is low-energy, they will pull you down. If you are near someone who is high-energy, they will pull you up. The more you are a positive, high-energy person, the more people want to be around you. When you become a more positive person, when you always focus on the sunshine and silver linings, people want to be around you.

It doesn't matter if you are out of touch with reality. It does not matter if you are dumb. It does not matter if you're ignorant. If you are happy, people want to be around you. Happiness trumps almost any other personality trait. Positivity is more important in friendships and relationships than intelligence and skills. That is how powerful it is. It's the prime trait that makes people want to be around you.

Reflection Questions

Answer the following questions in your Love Yourself Journal.

1. Which of the techniques and tips discussed above are you already using in your life? How effective do you find them to be? What will you do to use more of these tips and

improve their effect in your life in the future? What is your implementation strategy?

2. Which tip from above are you going to try first? Why? How are you going to do it? Why do you think it will work for you?

3. Did you find any of the tips or techniques surprising or shocking? Why? Was one of them a total surprise for you? Why or why not? Do you feel like there is one that might not work? It is okay to disagree with me. Be eloquent in your reasoning. Remember that this is a conversation, not a monologue. It's okay to have your own opinions.

4. How would you rate your self-esteem right now on a scale of one to ten? This is an answer that should be more than one word. Dig into your self-perception and be honest with yourself. We need this measurement so that we can then measure your success.

5. Take a look at that list of twelve different tips for improving your self-esteem. How many of them do you currently implement? Are you using all twelve of them, seven of them or none of them? When assessing your self-esteem, are you surprised by how many techniques you actually do not do? Are you surprised to discover that actually you don't practice high self-esteem?

6. Which of the tips do you think will be most effective for you? Which you think will best fit you? Why do you think it will work for you?

Self-Esteem Exercise

Now that we have our self-esteem baseline, choose at least five tips from the section above and spend the next week actively practicing them. Focus on improving yourself for the next five days. After you have completed your five days of work, answer these questions in you Love Yourself Journal:

1. Now that your high-self-esteem week is completed, is your self-esteem higher or lower? Did this exercise work for you? If you find that your self-esteem has not improved, is the problem that you need more time with these exercises or are they just not working right for you? Analyze your experience and write down your answers.
2. How would you rate your overall happiness over the last week – was it higher or lower than the week before?
3. Have people been treating you differently this week?
4. Were there situations that would have upset you in the past that didn't bother you this week?
5. Did the situations change or simply your perception of them?

11

CONFIDENCE ACCELERATOR

Y ou can't build high confidence without a foundation of strong self-esteem. It's easy to tell you to improve your self-esteem, but that's just words. There are a few more practical things you can do that will strengthen your self-esteem.

It starts with the correct mindset. If you integrate these three concepts, your self-esteem will be continuously hardening:

1. Step outside of your comfort zone and try new things.
2. Always seek to move forward. An example of this is to put yourself forward for a promotion or an advancement in the workplace.
3. Even though you are already great, there's always room for improvement! Be enthusiastic about self-improvement.

Confidence Improvement Exercises

Remember what I said about "faking it until you make it?" This is part of what I said about practicing confidence in order to become more intrinsically confident. Below are some exercises that implement this technique. You can pick and choose which ones you want to do, but you should make sure to do a number of them!

You might find some of these a little bit silly, but they are also fun. Don't assume that because they seem to focus on superficial things they will not be helpful. Small steps add up to much bigger changes.

1. Take a chance with your fashion. You can look good in lots of different styles. Don't restrict yourself or imagine that you only look good in certain things. If you want, you can begin by wearing different things only in the house.

I didn't share this story in the first three drafts of this book, but I think you deserve one more piece of gold. When I wanted to build up my self-confidence, I took this concept to heart. I had a pair of angel wings left over from that girl I was in love with who cheated on all her boyfriends. One night, I put them on under my jacket and went to a friend's birthday party.

Taking off that jacket was one of the hardest things I've ever done, but nothing else I've ever done has boosted my self-confidence so much so quickly. After doing that, so many small things stopped affecting me.

2. Put yourself forward more often. Don't hold yourself back because of fear of failure. Everyone fails sometimes, and that is only a step in the road to success. If don't yet believe in your abilities, simply pretend and act like you do. Go for promotions in the workplace and take up leadership roles.

3. Get involved in new activities and learn new things. The feeling of accomplishing things and gaining new knowledge will help to boost your sense of self-efficacy, and therefore your confidence.

4. Set goals and keep track of when you achieve them. Give yourself credit for everything that you achieve and pat yourself on the back.

5. Give yourself compliments and accept compliments from others. You deserve them!

6. Don't take criticism personally, but if it's constructive, do your best to learn from it.

7. Be assertive. Your ideas and opinions need to be heard.

8. Learn from the confident people you see around you. Observe them when you can and take tips from their approach to life.

9. Be positive and cheerful. And if you don't feel cheerful, remember our "fake it until you make it" tip.

10. Take care of yourself. A strong level of self-care is very important in building confidence.

Reflection Questions

1. Which of the above tips do you think you will find most helpful? Which of them have you used in the past? Did you give them a fair chance or did you give up too early?
2. How much of a role do you feel that confidence has played in your life? How do you feel that your life has been affected by a lack of confidence?

3. Have there been any opportunities in your life (for example opportunities in the workplace) that you have shied away from because of a lack of confidence in yourself and your abilities?
4. Are you excited about how a better level of confidence will help to improve your life?

12

BECOME CHARISMATIC

We are moving towards the end of this book, and we have accomplished a lot of amazing things together. Our goal is more than just to learn how to fall in love with yourself all over again. That is where this book begins, but it ends with becoming more charismatic, which is where people start to love you, want to follow you, and want to connect with you. This comes from the triumvirate of three key elements; self-confidence, passion, and honesty.

Throughout this book, we have put together these pieces and talked about finding things that you love to do, finding things that you are excellent at, being true to yourself, and boosting your confidence, self-esteem, and self-efficacy. We have worked on those pieces separately, and now we are going to bring them together and create someone that people are inspired by and want to connect with. The more you can implement these three pillars of an amazing personality, the more people will be drawn towards you.

Charisma Recipe

Let us talk about some specific elements of charisma – the final spices that we are going to add to our perfect dish of "charisma a la mode."

1. Be true to yourself. When I talk about honesty, it is not only about being honest with other people; it is also about being honest with yourself and admitting the things you like and don't like. Oftentimes, we are stuck in careers, relationships, and friendships where we are not meant to be, and because we are not in the right place, it is very hard for us to communicate those things. It is very hard to lead people when you're doing something you hate, but when you switch to a career that you love, you become far more magnetic.

When I began working for myself and I moved into something that I loved, my charisma went through the roof! I enjoyed working as a teacher for a while, but by the end of my ten years teaching around the world, I kind of hated it.

When you are a teacher, you have to teach the same lessons over and over again every single day. At one point, I was teaching twenty classes, and they were all having the same lesson every week. I would repeat myself over and over again every day, and I found it soul sucking, monotonous, and depressing. I hated it.

Perhaps if I had been teaching in a different system, where every week was a new adventure, and you were traveling along with your students, I might've enjoyed that more. That is not the style of teaching I was a part of. It was very hard for me to convince other people to follow me or want to become teachers when I didn't love my job that much. I was not being true to myself.

2. Allow yourself to flourish as a human being. The things that make you different are the things that make you great. There are hundreds of people teaching similar lessons to what I teach, but they are all

different people; that is what makes their lessons different. Two people can write the exact same book, but when you read both, you can't connect with one because you don't connect with the writer.

What separates me from other writers is not the content or the concepts. I have come up with my own ideas through my own creativity, but I am not so pretentious as to imagine that I have invented something completely new or that no one else ever thought of it before. I am sure that most of the content of this book can be found in other books, but taught in different ways, with different styles, by different unique teachers. What makes me special is my uniqueness, my story, my journey, the life I lead, and the people I connect with.

Defining your uniqueness and your passions will draw people to you. It doesn't matter what you are passionate about. What matters is how you talk about it and how you express yourself. The more passion you convey about a hobby, the more people will find you magnetic. It does not matter if your hobby is designing costumes for video game conventions, playing chess, or collecting comic books. The way you talk about it will affect the way people perceive it.

If you talk about your hobbies and your passions like something that you are ashamed of and you want to keep secretive, people will go, "Well, if he is not even proud of it, it must not be that cool." Your excitement is far more important than the actual hobby. It does not matter if people like actual activity; what they really want to see is how it makes you feel.

This is a powerful lesson if you can connect with it. You can enjoy doing anything, as long as you don't hide your joy, people will find it magnetic and charismatic. You are already doing things that other people would love to hear about, but you are afraid to talk about it, and that is holding back your charisma.

3. Cultivate enthusiasm for new experiences. The more you are enthusiastic about life, the better your life will be. One of the reasons people are drawn to me is that I am knowledgeable about thousands

of subjects. I have tried many different things, and I am always willing to try something new – even if I think I might not like it.

I always thought I would hate roller coasters as an adult because I hated them as a child. When I was living in Japan, I got trapped on a roller coaster for more than an hour. When they were locking me into the chair, they messed up my settings and made it so tight against my bones that they could not unlock it at the end of the ride. While the rest of my friends were standing around in horror, I was trapped on this rickety roller coaster wondering if that was the end of my days. I tried it once, and I don't ride roller coasters anymore. I paid my dues.

A willingness to try everything once is refreshing. As I get older, of course, I get more set in my ways, and I want to try new things less and less. Sometimes, my wife and children have to talk me into it, and I have to actively remind myself that trying new things is good. It's how we stay fresh. We need new experiences to keep our minds agile, strong, and young.

The most charismatic people are excited about life and about trying new things. They are not just excited about repeating things they have done over and over again. Very rarely will I watch a movie a second time. I am not looking to repeat experiences. What I am looking to do is have new amazing experiences. Going outside your comfort zone and trying new things will expand you in both areas.

I mentioned earlier the idea of trying a new hobby every week until you find the one. This is about pushing yourself outside your comfort zone. Your comfort zone is a barrier to your influence on the universe. If you have a small comfort zone, you influence a small part of the world. If you have a large comfort zone, you influence a larger part of the world. The more you expand your comfort zone, the more confident you will become.

4. Demonstrate empathy for other people. Empathy is where you care, understand, and feel what other people are going through. When someone is sad, you can actually feel their sadness; when someone is pained, you can feel that pain within you. The more you

feel what other people are feeling, the more charismatic you become. Who wants to be led by an emotionless robot? Followers want to believe that their generals and leaders care about them in a meaningful way.

Do you want to be led by someone who sees you as a piece on a chessboard or someone who agonizes over putting you in a dangerous situation, even when it's necessary? True leaders care about their soldiers, their followers, their supporters, and their team, and they pay attention to what they are going through in their condition. This is another area where it is tough because as we lead more people, there are always people on our team are going through something tough, which means we're always in a state of feeling bad.

Many leaders who distance themselves from their teams begin to burn off their empathy and emotions. They begin to block off those feelings so that they do not become distracted. This is something that you have to deal with as you become more of a leader. Do not block off your emotions now; wait until you get there, and only then deal with that problem.

5. Find something to believe in, and jump in with both feet. Maybe you have a political belief. Maybe you have an environmental belief or are part of a group, and you want to help a different charity. The more you become passionate about something in particular, the more people are drawn to you.

Find something that draws you. I am very passionate about helping people overcome emotional, personal, and career-related challenges. That is why all of my books follow the same thread. It is very easy for me to write a book when I am passionate about it.

I very much want to hear that your life is transformed by this book. That matters to me because I care about the results. I email back every person who emails me, from any of my books. When people read more of my books, they trust me more because they know I am serious about it. It is easier to trust someone who has true empathy for you and truly believes in your cause. If you want to check if that is true, just reply to one of my emails. Join my Facebook group and post a message; see what happens. You will hear from me.

Charisma Exercises

Break out the Love Yourself Journal; we are going to go through several exercises.

1. What does it mean to be true to yourself?

In your Journal, brainstorm and come up with some short ideas about what it means to be true to yourself. Maybe your measurement of true self can only be seen in test environments; you can only tell if someone is true to themselves when they are put to the test. Perhaps the only way to know if someone is a true friend is to put the relationship under stress.

It is easy to be friends when times are good; it is hard to be friends when times are tough. As you work your way through this activity, write down whether or not you think you are true to yourself. Have there been times when you have let yourself down?

2. What makes you unique?

The difference lies in what will make people connect with you and want to follow you. It is not the sameness. When you watch a movie and see those extras in the background, who are all wearing the same uniform and a look interchangeable, you find them uninspiring and insignificant; it is the characters who have speaking lines with individual and unique characteristics who make themselves unique. Those are the ones we follow and develop feelings for. We want to see them make it to the end of the movie.

What is it about you that is unique? What is special about you? I can try to lead by example here, and I think there are lots of things that are special about me; the way I lead my family, the way I care about my kids, the way I live my life, where I live my life, the way I have built my business, and how hard I strive to become a better person. All of these things make me unique. Other people have the same abilities and characteristics, but I mean a unique combination of them.

Make a list of your uniqueness and include any specific talents that you have. Maybe you have an amazing ability to do accents, or maybe you have amazing hearing. Make a list of all the different things that make you unique and great.

Perhaps my most unique talent is that I am a very good teacher. I am able to express wisdom and knowledge in a way that is not boring. Having worked as a teacher for a very long time, I discovered that this is pretty rare and valuable. I struggled as a student to connect with boring teachers and textbooks. That is why I work so hard to weave in story after story into to these lessons to ensure that you never find them boring. That is my greatest fear: once we start to lose interest, we start to lose the lesson.

3. Finding a cause.

What are some causes that you are interested in? I had certain causes that I was very passionate about when I was younger, and of course, a lot of them have evolved and moved into doing things that were not the original purpose of the cause. I was a big fan of blood drives. I still am. I think donating blood is a great cause, and it is very simple.

Where I went to high school, we were the only high school in the whole city that did not have a blood drive. I arranged our first ever blood drive. Of course, part of it was having something to put in my college resume, and part of it was working towards running for that student body election that I lost dramatically, but part of it was also that I thought it was important.

You can find one cause that works for you. Maybe you are passionate about adult literacy or diseases in Africa. It does not matter what it is. My passion now is about my family and the things I want to teach people. I write books that I want to help people with, so my work has become my cause in a sense. If you don't have a cause, spend some time brainstorming.

4. Walking in another person's shoes.

We are narcissists by nature. We only care about ourselves, and we can only imagine our own experience. It is very hard to imagine what other people are actually going through.

For this exercise, spend an entire day pretending you are someone else. Think about every aspect of their lives.

- What does it feel like when they go to work?
- What does it feel like talking to their boss?
- What does it feel like when they get home from work?
- What does it feel like to drive their car?

What we are trying to do is a forced empathy exercise, to learn what it's like to see the other person's side of the coin.

When we are talking to someone else, we are often so caught up in our own perspective that we forget that the other person has perspectives too. Spend some time imagining what it is like to live in someone else's shoes and write about it in your Journal. Write about their struggles or tribulations and their experience of the universe, and begin to expand your horizons in a meaningful way.

Charisma Case Study

Think of someone you personally know who is very charismatic, and then answer the following four questions.

1. What makes this person unique?
2. Do you feel that this person is true to themselves? Why? How

can you tell that they are true to themselves? How do they reveal that they are true to themselves?

3. Does this person have a cause that they passionately believe in? It does not have to be anything big or incredibly important to the world, but is there something in their lives that they believe in?

4. Do you think this person makes an effort to see the world from other people's point of view? Can you recognize the empathy in their lives? Can you see them empathizing with you? How? What are they doing that reveals they understand your experience of the world?

THE END OF THE LINE

We have covered so much territory in this book. It is almost unbelievable. What I would like you to do now is begin to look at how all these different lessons integrate and mingle together – how loving yourself is a core component of charisma; how falling in love with yourself and developing a passion for yourself is really important; how having high self-esteem is going to be one of the first building blocks to charisma, along with confidence; how believing in your ability to accomplish things and having empathy for other people will change your life.

As we worked on all these different traits of your personality, you have probably identified areas where you need to improve further, because everyone does. Even as I was writing this book, I mentioned a few areas where I felt like I can improve. It is important to understand that this is not a moment in time; this is a journey.

We are at the end of this book, but we are only at the beginning of your journey. What happens next will determine how effective this book is for you. I have shared all my lessons with you, and I am available to you. If you have more questions, you can join the Facebook group and ask me or email directly. I want you to succeed, and for that reason, I am willing to answer any questions and connect with you. This book is a cooperative journey. I took the first few steps, and now the ball is in your court. I am waiting to see what you do next.

The more you can develop your honesty, passion, and self-confidence, the more people will be drawn to you for a long time. If you have been cycling in a negative direction, we can reverse that now. You can move your way upwards. That is what I want you to work on. That is what I want you to believe. It is possible to improve a lot in life.

Charisma is a skill, not a talent; it is something you can improve. If that is the only lesson you take from this book, then this book has succeeded. If you worked your way through the Love Yourself Journal, whether you created your own journal or bought the one that I put together, you have gained a deeper understanding of yourself.

Work your way through the exercises over the next couple of weeks. Go out, do the activities, and write down the assessments. Watch your confidence grow. Before you doubt the techniques, please try them.

In a moment, you will have an opportunity to leave a review for this book. All I ask is that you are honest in your review. If you leave a bad review because you did not try any of the techniques as you did not think they would work, just say that, "I leave this book a bad review, even though I did not try any of the techniques." Yes, that is unfair, but at least have the courtesy to be honest.

If you did not try any of the techniques, if you read this book in a single day and did not write down a single activity, of course it won't work. If you buy a video game and read the instructions but never plug it into your system, it is not going to be very fun. Would you give a bad review to a video game you have never played?

If you spend the next few weeks trying the techniques and giving me one hundred percent and they don't work for you, then I deserve a bad review. That is fair. But when you try these exercises, really give it a hundred percent. Give it enough time to see how your charisma changes, and how the way people treat you changes.

I was painfully unpopular when I was younger, and now people listen to me when I speak. You can accomplish the exact same things.

I believe in you. You are an action-taker. The fact that you read this book all the way to the end shows me that you are serious.

Most people don't finish the books that they buy. This applies to every book out there; fiction and non-fiction, historical, even comic books don't get finished. You are different; you made it to the end, and that gets me excited. If you made it this far, there is a very good chance that you will continue this journey.

What I ask you to do is to keep me in your heart and keep this book as part of your journey. When you implement the lessons from this book, write about that in your reviews; write about that when you email me. When you post a review on Amazon, include a picture of that shiny bathroom you have taken control over. That will be our little inside joke that lets me know that you read this book.

I am excited about you being on this journey. You're not alone; you are a member of my tribe, and that is important to me. You can reach me in my Facebook group. All you have to do is click the link at the beginning or at the end of this book to join my tribe, and I will send you a direct invitation. You don't have to pay anything; you have already bought this book. Even if you acquired this book through Kindle Unlimited, that is fine. I put this book on Kindle Unlimited to reach as many people as possible.

All I ask from you is to reach out to me if you are having a tough day, if you are feeling stuck on one of the exercises, or if something is not working for you. I want to help you. I want you to succeed. Let us make this a cooperative venture.

Maybe for the first time in a long time, you are looking into the future with a smile on your face. If you are excited about the possibilities in front of you, instead of being stressed out about the mistakes behind you, if I have taken you that far on this journey, then I am excited!

I care about what you have to say, and I will react to it. If you email me and say, "Jonathan, if you write a book dealing with this specific issue that would really help me," then I will do that. I do that a lot. I love giving people what they need and what they want, and I love hearing back from you.

Thank you so much for being a part of this journey. I don't want to draw this conclusion too long, but I want to ask you once again to give this book one hundred percent and go for it! Maybe you have read books before on self-improving aspects of your life, but you never did the exercises. This is your chance to do something different. If you email me, I will reply; if you message me in the Facebook group, I will respond. If you do the exercises, your life will change. That is my promise to you.

Thank you so much for joining me on this journey, and I look forward to hearing about your massive successes.

MORE INFORMATION

T hroughout this book I mentioned other books, images, links, and additional content. All of that can be found at:

https://servenomaster.com/loveyourself

You don't have to worry about trying to remember any other links or the names of anything mentioned in this book. Just enjoy the journey and focus on taking control of your destiny.

LET'S SOAR TOGETHER

The hardest part of dealing with depression is going it alone. When you are in isolation, the night can seem so dark. Please join my FREE, private Facebook group filled with supportive people on the same path.

https://servenomaster.com/lovely

This is a great place to chat with me daily, share your experiences with the exercises and find a supportive group of people who are all on the same journey as you.

FOUND A TYPO?

While every effort goes into ensuring that this book is flawless, it is inevitable that a mistake or two will slip through the cracks.

If you find an error of any kind in this book, please let me know by visiting:

ServeNoMaster.com/typos

I appreciate you taking the time to notify me. This ensures that future readers never have to experience that awful typo. You are making the world a better place.

ABOUT THE AUTHOR

Born in Los Angeles, raised in Nashville, educated in London - Jonathan Green has spent years wandering the globe as his own boss - but it didn't come without a price. Like most people, he struggled through years of working in a vast, unfeeling bureaucracy.

And after the backstabbing and gossip of the university system threw him out of his job, he was "totally devastated" – stranded far away from home without a paycheck coming in. Despite having to hang on to survival with his fingernails, he didn't just survive, he thrived.

In fact, today he says that getting fired with no safety net was the best thing that ever happened to him – despite the stress, it gave him an opportunity to rebuild and redesign his life.

One year after being on the edge of financial ruin, Jonathan had replaced his job, working as a six-figure SEO consultant. But with his rolodex overflowing with local businesses and their demands getting higher and higher, he knew that he had to take his hands off the wheel.

That's one of the big takeaways from his experience. Lifestyle design can't just be about a job replacing income, because often, you're replicating the stress and misery that comes with that lifestyle too!

Thanks to smart planning and personal discipline, he started from scratch again – with a focus on repeatable, passive income that created lifestyle freedom.

He was more successful than he could have possibly expected. He traveled the world, helped friends and family, and moved to an island in the South Pacific.

Now, he's devoted himself to breaking down every hurdle entrepreneurs face at every stage of their development, from developing mental strength and resilience in the depths of depression and anxiety, to developing financial and business literacy, to building a concrete plan to escape the 9-to-5, all the way down to the nitty-gritty details of teaching what you need to build a business of your own.

In a digital world packed with "experts," there are few people with the experience to tell you how things really work, why they work, and what's actually working in the online business world right now.

Jonathan doesn't just have the experience, he has it in a variety of spaces. A best-selling author, a "Ghostwriter to the Gurus" who commands sky-high rates due to his ability to deliver captivating work in a hurry, and a video producer who helps small businesses share their skills with their communities.

He's also the founder of the Serve No Master podcast, a weekly show that's focused on financial independence, networking with the world's most influential people, writing epic stuff online, and traveling the world for cheap.

All together, it makes him one of the most captivating and accomplished people in the lifestyle design world, sharing the best of what he knows with total transparency, as part of a mission to free regular people from the 9-to-5 and live on their own terms.

Learn from his successes and failures and Serve No Master.

Find out more about Jonathan at:
ServeNoMaster.com

BOOKS BY JONATHAN GREEN

Non-Fiction

Serve No Master Series

Serve No Master

Serve No Master (French)

Breaking Orbit

20K a Day

Control Your Fate

Break Through (coming soon)

Habit of Success Series

PROCRASTINATION

Influence and Persuasion

Overcome Depression

Stop Worrying and Anxiety

Love Yourself

Conquer Stress

Law of Attraction

Mindfulness and Meditation Ultimate Guide

Meditation Techniques for Beginners

Social Anxiety and Shyness Ultimate Guide

Coloring Depression Away with Adult Coloring Books

Don't be Quiet

Seven Secrets

Seven Networking Secrets for Jobseekers

Biographies

The Fate of my Father

Complex Adult Coloring Books

The Dinosaur Adult Coloring Book

The Dog Adult Coloring Book

The Celtic Adult Coloring Book

The Outer Space Adult Coloring Book

Irreverent Coloring Books

Dragons Are Bastards

Fiction

Gunpowder and Magic

The Outlier (As Drake Blackstone)

ONE LAST THING

Reviews are the lifeblood of any book on Amazon and especially for the independent author. If you would click five stars on your Kindle device or visit this special link at your convenience, that will ensure that I can continue to produce more books. A quick rating or review helps me to support my family and I deeply appreciate it.

Without stars and reviews, you would never have found this book. Please take just thirty seconds of your time to support an independent author by leaving a rating.

Thank you so much!

To leave a review go to ->

https://servenomaster.com/lovereview

Sincerely,
Jonathan Green
ServeNoMaster.com

10601911R00066

Printed in Great Britain
by Amazon